# How Quiet Introverts Thrive in An Extrovert World

Learn How the Shy can Outsell Anyone, Succeed as an Entrepreneur, and Take Advantage to Win & Influence People & Friends - Improve Your Social Skills

**Samuel C. Larson**

© **Copyright 2019 - All rights reserved.**

The content contained within this book may not be reproduced, duplicated or transmitted without direct written permission from the author or the publisher.

Under no circumstances will any blame or legal responsibility be held against the publisher, or author, for any damages, reparation, or monetary loss due to the information contained within this book. Either directly or indirectly.

## Legal Notice

This book is copyright protected. This book is only for personal use. You cannot amend, distribute, sell, use, quote or paraphrase any part, or the content within this book, without the consent of the author or publisher.

## Disclaimer Notice

Please note the information contained within this document is for educational and entertainment purposes only. All effort has been executed to present accurate, up to date, and reliable, complete information. No warranties of any kind are declared or implied. Readers acknowledge that the author is not engaging in the rendering of legal, financial, medical or professional advice. The content within this book has been derived from various sources. Please consult a licensed professional before attempting any techniques outlined in this book.

By reading this document, the reader agrees that under no circumstances is the author responsible for any losses, direct or indirect, which are incurred as a result of the use of information contained within this document, including, but not limited to, — errors, omissions, or inaccuracies.

# Contents

Chapter 1:
Nothing Wrong with Being an Introvert _____ 1

Chapter 2:
Introvert Myths Debunked _____ 12

Chapter 3:
Dominate Life Even When Quiet and Shy _____ 19

Chapter 4:
What Your Competitive Edge Is _____ 27

Chapter 5:
Creating Chatter and Small Talk Without Being Awkward _____ 39

Chapter 6:
Leverage Charisma on Command _____ 48

Chapter 7:
Tips for Networking and Making Friends _____ 56

Chapter 8:
Survival Guide for Social Events _____ 66

Chapter 9:
Outsell the Extroverts _____ 75

Chapter 10:
Crush Your Competitors _____ 85

Chapter 11:
Make Yourself Known _____ 93

Chapter 12:
Persuade People Even When You're Nervous _____ 101

Chapter 13:
Understanding Other People's Emotions and Thrive _____ 109

Chapter 14:
Tips for the Sensitive and Shy _____ 116

# Chapter 1:
# Nothing Wrong with Being an Introvert

Being an introvert is not easy. People often misunderstand you and make an opinion about you even before they get to know who you truly are. There is a lot of pressure on introverts to become more outgoing and change the way they live only because society will not accept who they truly are. If you are an introvert and you are having a lot of problems dealing with it, then you need to read on. Just because you find staying in the confinement of your cubicle more comforting than talking loudly at your office meeting doesn't mean that something is wrong with you. An introvert can be just as productive and successful as an extrovert as long as they learn to prove themselves by taking the right steps.

You do not have to worry about changing your personality in order to fit in. Remember, some people were born to stand out and if being quiet makes you that person, accept it and learn how to make the most of it.

**The Extrovert Expectation**

One of the major problems of being an introvert is that you are normally surrounded by outgoing people who are social and have a certain expectation from you. Whether it's your work environment or the people you socialize with, there are certain expectations everyone has and they believe that you should live up to them even if you are not comfortable with it. There are some people who manage to effortlessly engage with others even if they haven't gotten to know them that well. This may seem really difficult for an introvert who struggles to strike a conversation even with someone they are familiar with.

Just because you cannot hold up your end of the conversation it doesn't mean that you are someone who should be targeted. Introverts need to learn how to deal with society and let them know that, while they are a little shy in comparison to the other people they know and it does take them a little bit longer to hold a conversation, it doesn't make them socially awkward. If you are an introvert do not be shy of who you are. Instead, try to convert your weakness into your greatest strength by showing people your true self rather than trying to be somebody you aren't.

### Self-Acceptance

Just because everybody does it, doesn't mean it is correct and that's exactly how you have to be. One of the biggest problems of society is that they look at an extrovert and keep them as their role model. They believe that these role models can strike conversations and be the center of attraction in every social gathering and that's exactly what everyone aspires to become. An introvert can also become a popular personality in the social circle once they learn that accepting their true nature can work in their favor.

Instead of trying to change the way you address situations and forcing yourself to get out of your comfort zone, you need to learn how to be comfortable in your own skin. It doesn't matter if you stand in one corner of a social gathering without striking a conversation with anyone. The very fact that you made an effort to get to the social gathering speaks volumes of you as a person. Introverts are not people who are quiet all the time. They are those people who are quiet when they are in front of strangers or people, they are not comfortable with. If you want to overcome this awkwardness in society, all you need to do is know how to be comfortable in your own skin. This will help you go places without trying to push yourself to do things that don't bring you any happiness.

### Don't be Misunderstood

Introverts are often misunderstood and believed to be people who tend to prefer spending time alone rather than socializing with the crowd. The truth is introverts are very creative and can come up with some of the best innovative solutions for various corporations and businesses by putting their mind to work in wonderful ways. Most introverts are known to think out of the box and while they do enjoy the solitude it doesn't mean that's what they represent. While an introvert enjoys spending time alone, it doesn't mean that they are alone all the time. It's just that they are comfortable with a certain amount of people whom they have known for a long time as opposed to an extrovert who finds comfort even with new people.

One of the best things about introverts is that their nature helps them to think before they take action and this is what reflects in the kind of work that they do. They are not hasty decision makers which means that there is less room for error with the kind of work that an introvert will complete. They also tend to get less distracted because small talk is something that they aren't into and they prefer privacy over openly sharing a lot of information about themselves.

Many people believe it's difficult to maintain a friendship with an introvert but the truth is the exact opposite. When you are looking for somebody to listen to you or share your secrets with, you will be able to do it a lot better with an introvert in comparison to an extrovert because introverts understand privacy and respect it. While you may think that they are a social misfit, the truth is they are quirky and their nature eventually tends to impress everybody who gets to know them. An introvert is not somebody who will be unable to discuss or hold up a conversation. While they may find it difficult to have a conversation with somebody new, once they begin having a conversation, they will be a lot of fun. An introvert is highly likely to become a very successful entrepreneur and a thoughtful leader.

**Introverts Are Loners**

## How Quiet Introverts Thrive in An Extrovert World

One of the biggest problems of being an introvert is that most people believe you are a loner who does not fit into a social group. The truth is introverts are known to maintain their distance in a large gathering because it takes them a while to open up. If people were a little more considerate, an introvert wouldn't feel so uncomfortable in new situations and they would manage to get along with people just as well. We will discuss more common introvert myths in chapter 2.

### Introverts Communicate Effectively

Contrary to belief, introverts manage to communicate very effectively and they put a lot of time and thought into the kind of communication they have. You an introvert will not send you an incomplete text message or have an incomplete conversation with you. If you are in a discussion with an introvert, they will give you their full attention and you can rest assured that your conversation will be one that is very meaningful and you will learn a lot. Yes, introverts do not like to engage in small talk but that doesn't mean that they don't like to have a conversation. They just don't like wasting time talking about things that are irrelevant or putting other people down. You're not going to come across an introvert who speaks ill of another person or who insults somebody. The sad part is, introverts are often put down by others just because they do not participate in negative gossiping. Introverts spend a lot of time on the positive aspects of life. They tend to grow and become more successful because negativity is not part of the agenda.

**Samuel C. Larson**

## Introverts Are Highly Successful

You will be surprised to see a number of great personalities who were introverts by nature. Some of the most prominent personalities in history and on television have been introverts and the reason they manage to become so successful is because they work and observe. They are gifted personalities who use their thought process into developing something positive and insightful rather than indulge in unnecessary drama. Introverts will always take themselves away from drama because that's not who they truly are. They are the first people to arrive for the meeting and they will always be most prepared for it.

An introvert is also the one who will be the best dressed and always on time. They also know exactly how to treat people with respect. While some people tend to make fun of the nature of an introvert, it is their humble behavior that helps them to go places. There is no denying that an introvert may not flourish in every industry but they try to give it their best. Even if you try to put them in front of an audience, as uncomfortable as they are, they will still try to do as much as they can to focus on the task at hand. An introvert may not be the best person for a face-to-face sale or a marketing job, but they are definitely the kind of person who you would want to give a motivational speech to a group of employees just before they head in to do something prominent for the business.

### How Quiet Introverts Thrive in An Extrovert World

Introverts can grow to be successful as long as they learn how to accept who they are and you need to do that if you want to become more confident. If you're an introvert there's nothing wrong with it. You don't have to worry about what society will say. All you need to do is stop pretending to be someone else and become the person you always wanted to be.

If you are an introvert then it's important for you to learn how to deal with the problems you face so that you are not socially awkward. You need to try and get comfortable even when you are in a social situation. Let's take a look at some of the problems that an introvert faces on a regular basis.

### Making Excuses to Leave a Party

Introverts often feel pressured into going to parties at work or in their social circle but they always wonder when they can escape from the scenario completely. It's normal for an introvert to feel out of place in a larger social gathering or when they are around too many people that they do not know because it's not easy for them to open up to somebody they just met. If you are forced to go for a party you can't avoid, it would be best to go with somebody that you know because it makes you feel more comfortable and you will be able to talk to someone during the party. Every introvert has a circle of people that they are close to and comfortable with. So, take your time to figure out your circle and try to have them around you during social gatherings or parties.

## Low on Energy After Regular Activities

One of the problems of being an introvert is that you tend to feel drained at the end of your regular routine because you always look for excuses not to spend time socializing with people outside of your social circle. While it's good to be who you are, you need to make a little effort to socialize with a few people and that means you making an effort to try to go outside and interact with people for a little while. The more you learn how to do this, the higher the energy levels will be and you will feel energized. One of the smartest ways to do this is to find yourself a hobby that you are truly passionate about. This could be anything from walking around the park or even getting yourself a dog to accompany you on your evening trails.

## Being Questioned About Being Quiet

As an introvert, you are often asked questions with regards to why you are not saying anything. The truth is it is difficult for you to start a conversation with somebody you aren't familiar with or make yourself part of a conversation that doesn't excite you and that is absolutely fine. However, when you are questioned about why you are so quiet, always let them know that you are fine and you just enjoy listening to the conversation because you're getting to learn something.

## Working on a Group Project

An introvert dreads working on a group project because they have to communicate with people, they might not know that well and they will need to work along with them. This can be in the form of an oral presentation or a research essay that you need to create for work, it is important for you to learn how to communicate with the people you are working with in order for you to get the project completed. If you are an introvert make sure that you find yourself a job that you truly love and you are passionate about because when you enjoy what you are doing, a group project will no longer matter to you since you will be more focused on getting the project completed successfully. It won't matter whether or not you have to communicate with new people.

## Try to Avoid Crowds

Introverts always look to stay away from large crowds because they dread having to start a conversation with people they do not know. If you find it difficult going to the grocery store when it's too crowded because you do not like too many people around or you would prefer to eat your lunch alone at your office desk then there's nothing to worry about. This is a common fear of an introvert and the only thing you need to do is try to slowly make an effort to be around people who you associate with as your friends. The reason it is important for you to not spend your life in isolation is because this can have a negative impact on your health and your overall life and that's not healthy.

## Having to Handle Phone Calls

Introverts normally cringe when they see the phone ringing because it means they have to pick up the phone and talk to the person on the other end. While you may avoid a call, you do not want to attend, you will also need to make a little effort to talk to people every now and then to let them know you are fine. Communicating with your close friends and family is essential for overall development and mental health so make sure you pick up the phone whenever you can. You should also surprise your friends and family by giving them a call every now and then just to check on them.

## Worry About Losing Your Friend

Introverts always fear that they will lose their friends and they have to deal with life all alone. The truth is that your friends mean more than you think. Introverts are true to themselves and they do not lie about anything and hence they make good friends. Whether someone is looking to you for advice or whether they want your opinion on something you'll always be honest with them which is why your friends will never let go of you.

## FOMO

If you have a fear of missing out then all you need to do is conquer your fear by addressing it. Whatever you fear you need to face it. Whether it means not being able to see your friends because you are missing out on social happenings, just make the effort to be there.

## Living with an Extrovert

As strange as it may sound, most introverts tend to find love in an extrovert and while they say that opposites attract, it could be a little

### How Quiet Introverts Thrive in An Extrovert World

difficult to live with an extrovert when you like to do the opposite thing. While your partner may want to go out and have a good time at a party, you may want to sit at home with a bowl of popcorn and watch a romantic movie. The reason a relationship of an introvert and an extrovert is so amazing is because they manage to balance things out and get the best of both worlds. Don't look at your relationship as a problem in your life but rather look at it as a learning experience for both partners and try to bring out the best in each other.

## Chapter 2:
## Introvert Myths Debunked

People look at introverts as a different category of people and they believe that certain characteristics of introverts are true. These assumptions about introverts are usually made on the basis of their interaction with others and their behavior. However, some of these myths are not true and stereotyping introverts on the basis of these myths is just not fair. Here we bust a few myths about introverts.

**Introverts Are Shy**

A shy person is someone that is usually scared of interacting socially and that person is not necessarily an introvert. Yes, introverts avoid social interaction but not because they are shy. It's because it drains them of their energy. This is because of the extra effort they need to interact with people and this agitation is usually misinterpreted as being shy. A shy person usually avoids any kind of social interaction since they are afraid of people's perception about them and they are just afraid of not being accepted at all. When it comes to an introvert, there is no fear and their lack of social interaction is often misjudged. The fact remains that a number of extroverts are also shy when it comes to social interaction.

## Introverts Do Not Like People

That is definitely far from the truth. Introverts, similar to extroverts, love people around them. The only difference between an introvert and an extrovert is the number of people that they socialize with. Introverts usually choose quality over quantity while an extrovert would choose the other way around. An introvert usually loves to hang out with a small group of people rather than attending a large lavish party. Their idea of a conversation is a one on one interaction rather than a group discussion. Introverts are loyalists and they will stay true to their friends. Just because an introvert does not hang out with as many people as an extrovert does, it doesn't mean that they do not like people. They just choose their company wisely.

## Introverts Do Not Have Social Skills

Introverts are more than capable of having excellent social skills. Some introverts are known to be extremely charming and if you wouldn't know the other person was an introvert, you would mistake them for an extrovert. If an introvert doesn't have too much of an option but to interact socially, he or she would do so with a lot of energy. However, the time taken for an introvert to recharge once they have socialized is a lot more than an extrovert.

## Introverts Are Not Able to Provide Any Ideas or Give Valuable Thoughts

This is another area about introverts that is usually wrong. Just because a person is quiet it doesn't mean that he or she has nothing to contribute. There is a very wrong misconception in society that the person that talks the most has the best ideas. However, more often than not we realize that the person that speaks a lot tends to speak unnecessary words. An introvert chooses to keep a low profile because they do not feel the need to express all their ideas and thoughts. Introverts also find it difficult to express themselves and this is the reason their ideas are usually suppressed. It takes them a lot of time to open up and speak to the person sitting opposite them. If you do not give them that time and you move very swiftly ahead with the conversation, you would assume that the person has nothing to say.

## Introverts Love Being Alone

Yes, introverts do require a lot more alone time as compared to extroverts. However, that doesn't mean that they love being alone at all times. Introverts also look for intimacy and soulful conversations however that is only with a group of specific people. Introverts also go through loneliness and depression if no one approaches them or speaks with them. If you see an introverted person, do not wrongly assume that the person doesn't want to interact with you. They just choose not to because they are not comfortable with you and they have their own circle of friends and family members they would love to interact with.

## Introverts Do Not Know How to Have Fun

While an extrovert may show a lot of excitement towards a certain activity, an introvert tends to feel drained by the same activity. This is because introverts do not usually enjoy big parties or extravagant outings. But that doesn't mean that they do not know how to enjoy themselves. Introverts love to travel, dance, go on adventures with close friends and drink a lot but they do it in their own way.

## Introvert Often Tend to be Depressed

This is something that is related to the point of introverts being alone. Just because introverts are seen as people that want to be alone, people usually assume that they are undergoing a lot of depression. While an introvert will be withdrawn from the rest of the world and will keep in touch with a few friends and family members, it doesn't necessarily mean that they are depressed. There could be a very good possibility that they are drained and are disconnecting from the rest of the people until they regain their energy. Introverts have an excellent sense of imagination and they usually are a lot of fun when you get to know them better.

## There Aren't Many Introverts Out There

If you thought that introverts made up only a very small population of the earth's surface then you are wrong. There are a lot more introverts than you can imagine and, in some places, they usually make up about 35% to 40% of the population. The reason people do not notice an introvert is because they tend to keep to themselves and usually go unnoticed. Some introverts even pose as extroverts and try to fit into society without being judged.

## Introverts Always Prefer Listening

Yes, introverts do tend to listen a lot more than they speak however that doesn't mean that they do not enjoy speaking. People often misunderstand introverts and they assume that they just want to listen. Have you ever stopped and considered that an introvert may have dreams and passions of their own and they would love to speak to someone about it? An introvert has to deal with a lot of adjustment and this is the reason they usually feel drained out and choose to stay silent most of the time.

## Introverts Never Get Angry When Interrupted

This is where a lot of people are wrong. You will notice that people get very aggressive when talking to an introvert and they usually try to suppress their voice. The reason introverts do not usually speak back is because it takes a lot of time before they say anything. Extroverts usually consider their silence as an invitation to speak and they make it a habit to cut off the introverts while they are speaking.

## Introverts Are Very Rude

Introverts are probably the first to leave a party or the first to exit a social gathering. They do not like talking over the phone and in person, and this can usually be perceived as being rude. They usually take a lot of time to settle down and speak to a person regularly and until that happens, they will be looked upon as rude.

## Introversion Can be Treated

This is the assumption that people make regarding introverts. Just because they are quiet and keep to themselves, people think that they need 'fixing'. Most people usually try to cure introverts and turn them into extroverts. They do not look at the value the introverts bring into their lives.

## Introverts Are Usually Very Judgmental

The silent nature of an introvert makes others assume that they are being judged by that person. However, an introvert is just like any other normal human being and just because a person is silent it doesn't mean that they are judging you. Just like extroverts, introverts also love daydreaming and listening to music while going about their daily work. However, trying to fix introverts can be a futile attempt.

## Introverts do Not Have a Lot of Emotions

While introverts may not be able to share their enthusiasm or act surprised, it doesn't mean that they do not feel these emotions. Introverts have a lot of feelings and they are just not able to express it in the way you and I would. They usually do not express their emotions because they do not trust everyone around them. An introvert would be open only with the person that he or she trusts and this is when you see an introvert bloom.

# Chapter 3:
# Dominate Life Even When Quiet and Shy

The ability to stay calm and not say a word even when people around you are chaotic and noisy is something only an introvert can do. People often believe that an introvert loses out on an opportunity because they are not confident enough to take a step ahead and achieve their desired goals. The truth is that when it comes to focusing on a task at hand and proving their value, an introvert manages to do it more effectively in comparison to an extrovert because of the amount of dedication they put into the task.

Attention is something that is really important when it comes to getting a job done effectively and one of the reasons why introverts are so good at whatever they do is because they do not tend to shift focus and usually pay a lot of attention to whatever it is, they are doing. Since an introvert does not pay too much attention to small talk and indulge in gossip, there is a less chance that they would be very interested in a conversation that is not going to be fruitful in any way. While most of their colleagues invest a lot of time in checking out insignificant facts about other co-workers, an introvert will not engage in that sort of conversation and would rather focus on proving to be an asset to the organization.

The ability of an introvert to manage to focus on task doesn't only show up when they are in a workplace, it is something that has been with them all their life. An introvert will also manage to get their school and college homework done on time and in a precise manner because they don't have a lot of distractions to deal with. It is easy for an introvert to convert a lot of their energy into positive energy and do something significant with it. While an extrovert may waste a lot of time having a random conversation or socializing with new people, introverts focus on what actually matters and helps them to grow and become successful. While there are a number of people who believe that an introvert will not be able to make it big, the truth is the chances of an introvert becoming successful are just as high as that of an extrovert. Moreover, since they don't need to put in too much effort to avoid distractions, it makes them stronger candidates.

A lot of people believe that introverts are not dominating and they are very submissive when it comes to decision making. This is where most people go wrong. While an introvert does not speak a lot, the silence is often their weapon. Staying quiet doesn't necessarily mean that they agree with everything you have to say. When there is a relevant conversation and something that matters, they will voice their opinion. Do not give in to the idea of being able to dominate an introvert just because they work with you. You should know that they are just as strong headed as you are and they will not give in to something they do not believe is right. If you are an introvert and you often fear that you will not be able to succeed in your workplace or take your career to a higher path then here are a few tips for you to help you stay confident with who you are and use your silence and devoted attention to your benefit.

## Learn More About Yourself

Introverts usually label themselves as an introvert without figuring out how introverted they actually are. There are some introverts who just find it difficult hanging out with new people but are very comfortable talking to a group of people to socialize with on a regular basis. There are introverts who hate the idea of having a conversation with people, even those that they've known for a long time and try to avoid conversations altogether. If you want to do well in your career you have to come to terms with the fact that you cannot avoid conversations completely and it has to be a part of your regular life. While you may not be able to start a conversation initially, it's always good for you to start being a part of every conversation at work that is related to the kind of job that you do, so you know exactly what's happening and you are able to put your point of view across the table when necessary.

If you are not confident about talking to people in a conference room or during a meeting you will have to practice this skill. You are bound to be nervous and you will also get jittery just before you step into the meeting room but over a period of time, you will realize that this becomes a regular part of your routine. Eventually, it won't make you as uncomfortable as it did on the first day. Take time to understand your level of introverted behavior so you are able to rectify the places where you are a little weak. There is no denying that an introverted person will take a while to open up and start talking. However, the sooner you address this problem the easier it will be for you to deal with it and you will manage to come up with a solution that helps you grow your career and achieve success without any problems.

## Appreciate Yourself

One of the biggest problems of an introvert is that they constantly underestimate what they can do and they always believe that they are destined for failure. Instead of worrying about how you will fail because of not being able to hold up your side of the conversation you should focus on improving your skills. One of the best things about being an introvert is that you get to play to your strength. Every morning when you wake up you should remind yourself you need to do your job and you will try to do a lot better so you can actually move towards becoming successful.

While people believe that an introvert cannot be a strong leader the truth is when you have to work with a certain amount of people and you get familiar with them, you manage to be a more respected and stronger leader in comparison to an extrovert. This is because of your nature of being a little reserved, managing to maintain cordial respect, and a little distance which is necessary for people to learn to respect and be a little scared of you. When you take up the role of a leader you cannot be friends with your co-workers and this is something that an introvert can pull off really easily. This is the main reasons why most leaders, scientists, and innovators are introverts. If you think you will not be able to do something, look back at history, see the number of people who made a name for themselves and you will realize that they were all introverts. You have what it takes to be a strong leader, an entrepreneur, and a successful businessman so don't let your behavior or lack of social skills pull you down. You will manage to become successful in what you do when you put your heart to it.

## Choose One Uncomfortable Act and Attempt it

There are different things that would put you outside your comfort zone depending on what kind of an introvert you are. Begin by making a list of things that make you feel anxious and stressed. Once you have a list of things you know will stress you out, make sure that the list includes things that are not as stressful to do. Each day pick one task you think you will manage to achieve depending on how you feel. The key is to not push yourself to do something extremely uncomfortable on days when you do not feel good because you may set yourself up for failure. Instead, each morning looks at the list and ask yourself 'Am I going to be able to achieve this today?' And if you think you can, attempt it. For example, your list might include going to a nightclub on your own and talking to strangers. While doing this suddenly may seem a bit weird, you can start by going to a local restaurant or a coffee shop and chatting with a random stranger. See how you are feeling, and then take it forward one step at a time. It is important to keep pushing your limits and don't quit at the slightest feeling of discomfort.

You will not be successful all the time and there will be moments when you experience cold feet and you completely give up the attempt and that's normal! You're human and everyone fails once in a while but that's how you start learning to improve towards success. Don't push yourself to attempt the same task for two days in a row because that would also stress you out. Give yourself a break every now and then and tell yourself that if I did not succeed at first, it doesn't mean I am not destined to do it. You need to tell yourself that you just need to try another day.

If you are looking to improve at what you do and achieve success the one thing you should never do is de-motivate yourself. Being an introvert is in your nature and it's not something you can change. Instead, what you can do is enhance your personality. Stop blaming yourself for the choices you make or the decisions you take. Instead, focus on how you will enhance your skills to be a more people's person without pushing your limits.

## Reading

### How Quiet Introverts Thrive in An Extrovert World

This may come as a surprise to you, but reading is a great way to help you learn and tell you what to do when you have no idea how to move forward. When you read, you learn a lot about different things and this will increase your knowledge. You need to learn more in order to talk about these topics in public and strike a conversation when necessary. If there's one thing you should always remind yourself, you need to be happy with who you are. When you accept this, you will start feeling positive and move forward on the path of becoming successful because you will stay focused at what you do and you won't let negative things come in your way. Just because you are quiet doesn't mean you can't achieve what you want. Reading self-help books and positive books can help you achieve a lot in life and that's the reason reading is so essential. For example, self-help books help you to get a rationalized answer to your behavior and offers solutions to help deal with the various problems you face on a regular basis. If you suffer from anxiety issues and you hate stepping up in front of a crowd, reading self-help books on dealing with anxiety will help you not only to deal with your issues but will also help you to understand how important it is for you to adopt a positive attitude, face the most challenging situations with a brave approach, and have a comfortable feeling. You can use the steps mentioned in the book to your advantage and learn how to deal with various situations in a better way.

No matter what phase of your life you are in, you need to always remember that you need to be comfortable in your own shoes and only then will you be able to improve yourself as a person. Overcoming shyness does not necessarily mean you have to change your personality completely. It means you have to learn to deal with social situations that are important and help you to change the kind of growth and success that you are aiming at. In case you are an anxious introvert, where you find it difficult even stepping into a room filled with people, the smart thing for you to do would be to seek assistance from a counselor or somebody who can help you overcome your anxiety. They can assist you in becoming more confident and able to deal with your anxiety.

# Chapter 4:
# What Your Competitive Edge Is

It is a noisy world out there and for an introvert, it often gets very intimidating because they believe that they have nowhere to go or voice themselves. If you are an introvert and you are worried about not being successful because you believe you lack a competitive edge then you should know that an introvert has as much to offer as an extrovert. Just because someone is loud, it is not necessary they will become successful. Being loud is usually not the best way to go about things. Providing results is something that an introvert can be more consistent with, considering the fact that they stay focused easily and do not drift away to indulge in socializing at the workplace. While an extrovert may believe that they are managing to do a great job at their workplace by keeping everybody involved in conversations, there are certain tasks only an introvert can be a pro at and this is why they manage to do the job a lot better. In case you are wondering what, an introvert can bring to the table, then here are a few facts about introverts that will amaze you.

**Introverts are Very Inquisitive**

An extrovert is generally confident in comparison to an introvert and that's the reason they don't invest a lot of time in observing what's happening around them. They are engrossed in many conversations and this would usually mean there is a lack of focus in whatever they do. Introverts, on the other hand, prefer to spend time observing what's going on and soak up as much information as they can. They are aware of a certain situation in comparison to the others at the workplace because they are usually calmer and more focused on understanding the job at hand. In a meeting room where there are a bunch of people trying to understand instructions, an introvert will manage to get the instructions perfectly sorted out because they are focused on that particular information and they are trying to get as much out of it as possible.

They are also keen observers and they focus on what's going on around them which helps them to keep track of progress at the workplace. When an introvert is leading a team, they manage to deliver instructions very precisely to the team and this helps them to get the job done on time and in a specific way that actually works out to the benefit of the organization. Their inquisitive nature helps them to focus on the minute details of the task that make it that much better. This also helps to reduce the number of mistakes that one would make while completing the task and it helps to get the job done faster, in a calm and composed manner, rather than in a rushed situation which is more common when extroverts are involved.

## Introverts Shine When Put in the Spotlight

Just because someone is shy, it does not necessarily mean that they will not be able to perform well. Introverts actually excel at performing in a number of things and this includes the kind of work that they are handed. At the job, an introvert will focus to get it done precisely and in the right manner because they do not like mistakes and they have more energy to focus on the minute details that can help enhance the quality of work they deliver. Most introverts have a lot of power to impress people when it is their time to shine. Introverts know exactly what needs to be done to get the job completed well and when they have to work a little harder, they do it beautifully.

Don't underestimate your skills because when you are put to the test you will start performing like you never thought possible. In order for an introvert to do well, they only need to make sure that they get a job that they love doing and they will love working on a daily basis. When you're passionate about something you will push yourself to limits you never thought possible and you will do things you never imagined. So do not hold back because when it comes to performing not only will you do well but you will also surprise the people around you.

## Introverts Have Their Boiling Point

Introverts may come across as calm people but that does not mean that you can challenge them and push their buttons too much. It is common for people to bully an introvert because they believe that they can get away with it but the truth is that if you try too much, you may end up on the wrong side of the table with an introvert and that isn't a nice place to be. An introvert may be socially awkward and may not manage to pull off a conversation in front of a group. They may even come across as soft-spoken but when they get upset and when you push them over the edge, you will see a side of them you never thought existed. This is something you need to be aware of when you are working alongside an introvert in the capacity of a team member.

One of the reasons an introvert can also be an amazing leader is because they know exactly how to balance the good with the bad and give their team members a challenge to work towards. Since introverts so not waste too much time in focusing on the unnecessary drama with the team, the team starts to be more focused as well and this automatically increases the productivity as well as the quality of work delivered by the entire team. As calm and quiet as they may look, an introvert can be an extremely tough boss to satisfy and this pushes the people under them to work that much harder. Not only do introverts focus on getting good things done in their own they also strive to make people working under them a lot better.

## Introverts Are Competitive

Yes, an introvert can be much more competitive than an extrovert. Introverts just don't show their competitive streak because they are calm and they stay focused on what needs to be done rather than showing people how it's done. While everyone at the office may try to prove they are doing better than the others by trying to give out hints about the work that they got done, introverts simply wait till the end of the task and only deliver results that will shock people. Introvert sometimes obsessively focus on getting something done correctly and while this may seem like a bad thing, it works out to the benefit of the organization because they do not want to deliver anything that is short of perfect.

While introverts take a little time to blend into an organization, once they do, they have a strong stand and they prove how important and valuable they are to the organization by delivering results that are better. One of the best things about an introvert is that they spend a lot of time gathering information. This helps them to become stronger at what they know and use that information against others. While you may believe that an introvert is easy competition, the truth is that they are probably the strongest competition you have to face because they have paid a lot of attention to every little detail and they will use that to their advantage.

## They Have Fun

A lot of people believe that an introvert is a boring person and they are also loners. The truth, however, is that an introvert is anything but a loner and in fact, they spend a lot of time enjoying themselves and socializing. The only difference between an introvert and extrovert is that an introvert will only show their wild side to people whom they trust and have spent a lot of time with as opposed to an extrovert who manages to deal with people they recently met. The truth is an introvert is safer because they will not go out with a random stranger and get drunk. Introverts have a comfort zone and they tend to include people inside their comfort zone in order to have fun. Once the introverts get to know others, not only do they manage to go out for adventures and do crazy stuff but they also do things that other people would never expect them to do.

The big difference between an introvert and extrovert is extroverts tend to follow a pack, but introverts make decisions because they try out new things and surprise people around them.

Introverts are actually more connected with their feelings than other people are and this is why they are amazing at a number of things that they do. If you are wondering why introverts are so amazing and why you shouldn't change who you are then you should know that there are some things that introverts do amazingly well.

### Being an Amazing Listener

An introvert can spend a lot of time listening to conversations that people have and pay attention to every little detail of the conversation without getting bored. Extroverts are eager to start their end of the conversation without paying too much attention to the complete conversation but an introvert, on the other hand, chooses to listen patiently. They tend to listen to everything and only once they have understood their side of the story completely will they analyze and then come up with a solution or advice that can prove to be beneficial.

You don't need to worry about an introvert not paying attention to your conversation because they look you in your eye and understand every little word that you say. If there is something that they don't understand they will ask you and will make sure that they get all the details that are necessary for them to come up with a calculated solution or advice that will prove to be beneficial.

## They Are Sensitive

An introvert is highly sensitive and they are aware of your feelings because they are intuitive people. Just because an introvert doesn't socialize does not mean that they do not understand what you are feeling. This is why it is easy to connect with them because they are aware of how to deal with tough situations and they can provide comfort.

## They Are in Touch with Their Own Feelings

Introverts know exactly what they are feeling and they know when they need to move away from certain people or situations if they feel uncomfortable. An introvert is the last person to apologize for the way they feel. They are comfortable with who they are. It takes a while for an introvert to socialize and when they are not enjoying themselves when they are socializing, they will stop making an effort to stay a little longer just to please people. They have their feelings in mind and they pay attention to the need to feel good rather than try to make others feel good just because of their presence. While introverts know exactly when to leave a certain situation or person, they never hurt them while doing so. An introvert will not come out in the open and say that they are bored or that they are not happy being there. Instead, they will come up with an excuse that will make the person feel that the introvert genuinely needs to leave the scene.

## Me Time

Introverts know the importance of spending time with themselves and they are comfortable being alone from time to time. While this seems like a problem, the truth is that an introvert tends to be more independent when compared to people who always depend on others to get stuff done. Whether it is something as simple as heading to work on their own or even taking a holiday alone, they tend to be more on their toes to get it done rather an extrovert who usually plans such things with a lot of people in mind. While it's all about socializing for an extrovert, for an introvert it's all about how they will feel and whether or not it will make them feel better. They prioritize tasks depending on their importance and while you may believe this is selfish, it is actually one of the best things to do because they do not have frustrations or unfulfilled wishes just because they had to depend on another person. They go ahead and get it done because they wanted to and not because somebody else wanted them to.

## They Cultivate Healthy Relationships

Introverts take a long time to build a relationship with somebody they can trust and they do not just give in to someone the first time they meet them. This gives them time to analyze and observe the person they plan on getting into a relationship with and only once they are comfortable with the person will they take the next step ahead. While this may seem like a long and tedious task it proves to be highly beneficial because an introvert is less likely to have his or her heart broken as compared to an extrovert who has their heart on their sleeve. While an introvert may struggle with self-esteem, when they find somebody who understands what they need and supports them, they tend to become stronger and more confident in their own skin rather than trying to be somebody else.

## They Love Animals

This may seem irrelevant but somebody who loves animals is always a good person by heart. Introverts are usually inclined towards animals and they shower a lot of love towards them for various reasons. To begin with, an animal does not need you to have a conversation with them and they will be just as comfortable by your side without saying a word as they would be to go out with you for a walk in the park. Introverts enjoy the company of an animal because they know that they will not have to worry about trusting them or getting to know them before they can be comfortable with them. If you are an animal person and you have an introvert as a friend, it is a great way to break the ice. Animals also work really well for introverts to learn how to come out of their shell because it can be a great conversation starter.

## Deeper and More Meaningful Conversations
Small talk is not part of the plan when it comes to an introvert and if they start a conversation with someone it is usually a deep and meaningful conversation. While a lot of people believe that they will get bored by spending time with an introvert the truth is that they have so much to talk about and they talk about it with so much enthusiasm and passion that you can never get bored with them.

## They Think Before They Speak
One of the best things about an introvert is that they will never say unnecessary things that may make you feel bad about your feelings. They take a while to decide what they want to say, planning the statements in their head before speaking it out loud. When you are in a relationship with an introvert you are less likely to break out into fights due to something that your partner has said because an introvert always makes calculated decisions and only says what is necessary in the right way. It's very unlikely for an introvert to use bad language or raise their voice and this makes it very easy to communicate with them even if the situation is difficult. Introverts usually do not enjoy drama and that's how they expect others to behave when around them. They do not encourage unhealthy gossip or foul language which makes them better people.

## They Enjoy Nature

Introverts enjoy spending time outdoors and while a lot of people believe that they are loners and like to spend time inside, the truth is they enjoy going out for a trek and even sitting around in a garden or among the trees. Introverts do not enjoy socializing and are usually surrounded by people that matter a lot and they love spending time with. They also dislike going out for crowded parties and getting drunk in the middle of the night. They would love doing something a lot more meaningful such as a lunch picnic with family and close friends or a nature trail with their loved ones. While it seems boring when you are a little younger, once you reach a certain age you realize just how beautiful it is to spend your time in nature rather than attending a crowded party with drunk people.

## They Are Creative

One of the best things about an introvert is that they are really creative and they can come up with ideas that are brilliant and very innovative. The reason an introvert is able to do this is because they spend so much time analyzing every situation that they cover up every nook and corner of the job. This enables them to come up with plans that are interesting and creative. They also have a lot of energy in them that they focus on the job at hand and it helps their imagination to go wild.

While people look at introverts as people who don't like to socialize and are antisocial, the truth is an introvert knows how to balance work and play a lot better in comparison to the others and they know exactly when they need to get home. Introverts are generally more rested and active during the day because they do not let unnecessary drama get the better of them. They are more mature when it comes to making decisions and they spend the time to think about what is right and wrong before they actually act upon it.

# Chapter 5:
# Creating Chatter and Small Talk Without Being Awkward

It's no secret that introverts try to avoid making small talk as much as possible and while this is healthy for their productivity, it isn't something that they can avoid all through their life. While you try to stay out of irrelevant conversations as much as possible, you still need to make small talk with people when you run across them in the hallway or even when you are standing in line to grab a cup of coffee.

While there are a number of introverts that manage to pull off small talk without too much struggle, there are also some who find it extremely uncomfortable to open up to people when exchanging pleasantries or asking them how the day is going. This makes it difficult for them to adjust in a professional scenario. If you are wondering what to do in order for you to start making small talk with people then here are a few tips and tricks that will help you.

### Lowering Anxiety Levels
When it comes to small talk, introverts tend to get stressed and their anxiety levels start hitting the roof. While some people just find it

difficult to indulge in small talk, there are others who completely avoid the situation. Being an introvert is easy as long as you learn how to deal with situations that make you feel uncomfortable and make yourself comfortable in situations that you have to face on a regular basis.

Question yourself as to why you do not want to go in front of a group of people and try and find the answer for it. If the reason you're avoiding people is that you simply do not like to have a conversation with them, then you need to tell yourself that this is part of socializing that is important. You need to learn to do it if you want to maintain a cordial relationship with everyone you work with. Indulging in small talk doesn't necessarily mean asking them about irrelevant stuff. It can simply mean greeting them and enquiring how they are doing. If you are not comfortable talking about other people or situations that do not matter to you, you can always excuse yourself after greeting somebody. It is healthy to talk to the people you work with and even if this means indulging in a little small talk; it is something that you need to learn to do. This is because it will help control your anxiety levels and this not only helps you to overcome your fear of talking to new people, it makes you a little more confident.

## Be Purposeful

When someone strikes a conversation with you, do not approach the situation with a dull mood. Instant try to figure out what they are talking about and if its negative thoughts and attitude, then simply try to convert it into something more positive and fruitful. You need to start learning how to control conversations and talking about things that you would rather spend time discussing than talking about things that have no relevance in your life whatsoever. When you stop people from talking down to you or talking about negative things around you, they will eventually stop doing it completely and while you will still interact with these people, they will not waste your time bringing up a conversation you do not like. The reason it is important for you to have small talk is because you will learn to tell people what is important to discuss and you will try changing the way they think. Although this may seem like a really small step it works wonders to change the attitude of a person and when somebody begins doing things with a positive approach it turns out to be more fruitful and beneficial.

## Channeling Your Curiosity

An introvert is generally a very curious person and this means that while they may not be able to strike a conversation instantly they most definitely have a ton of ideas in their head. Even when an introvert asks someone 'how are you doing?', they also want to get other information out of them such as 'how was your weekend?' and 'what is going on at the work front?'. While introverts do not like to waste time on unnecessary information, they are always curious to gather information that can benefit them. They are the kind of people who look for positive interactions to develop future conversations that will benefit a lot of people. When an introvert strikes a conversation that they are interested in, they start focusing on the conversation with enthusiasm and they also contribute towards the conversation in a very effective manner.

## Ask Questions

As difficult as it may be to begin a conversation, it has to start sometime. Asking questions is a great way to begin a conversation because this helps you to get a response from the person and that helps you to get a little more comfortable with the conversation. The biggest fear of an introvert is that a conversation will not have any flow and once you ask a question you may not get an answer to it. The truth, however, is that when you ask a question, irrespective of what kind of question it is, you will definitely get a response so make an effort to ask a question as a conversation starter. Something as simple as asking them how they are doing or asking someone who has returned recently or resumed work after a sick leave whether they feel better are great ways to begin a conversation. It also helps you to create a bond with the people that you work with which is essential. When you start getting comfortable with the people around you, it becomes easier for you to work when you need to do a certain project as a team.

## Increase the Kind of Information You Provide

One of the biggest mistakes an introvert makes is to try and keep their responses as short as possible. Introverts will usually respond to questions like 'how are you?' with one-word answers such as fine or good. While their response is appreciated, apart from providing one-word answers you should also try to add a little more by letting them know about your plan or reciprocating by asking them how they are doing. If you begin the conversation then try something different like asking them about their plans for the weekend or even some personal information like where they are originally from.

While all of this information may seem extremely irrelevant to you it's the kind of information people want to know about you too and when you begin a conversation, they will definitely respond by asking you the same questions. It easier for you to learn more about people and this helps you to establish a more comfortable zone at work. The sooner you learn how to get comfortable with the people you work with, the more you look forward to spending time at work and this will encourage you to focus better on the kind of things you do rather than getting anxious the minute you spot people you are not comfortable talking to.

## Strengthen Conversations

Once you learn how to strike a conversation with someone and make small talk you, need to then take it to the next level by trying to increase the duration of the conversation and get more details about the person. While this is not necessary it is always better to do this because it helps you get comfortable with a high position and becoming a leader at your job. When you control people under you, you need to get to know them well and asking various questions throughout your professional life will help you do this in a better manner and will prepare you for what lies ahead. If you want to achieve success by doing what you love, you must make sure you get comfortable in the workspace so you are not in for a shock when you are required to speak to people suddenly.

The more you talk to people through one-on-one conversation, the more comfortable you will get and this will make it easier for you to speak to them. This will ensure that you are always in a room surrounded by a lot of people that you've already spoken to in the past as opposed to speaking in a room full of strangers. It also becomes easier for you to talk to people you've already spoken to because you can address them by name and start a conversation about something that relates to them. Not only does this help to grab the attention but it also makes them more focused on what you are saying.

## Start Smiling Often

One of the biggest problems of being an introvert is that you are often passed off as someone who has a bad attitude. Just because you don't like talking to people don't mean you are a snob and you need to let people know that. If someone starts rolling their eyes the minute, they see you, it's only because they believe that you do not like talking to them or that they are not worth your time. When you spend a lot of time with people in the same environment it is important to get along with them. Just because they believe that you are a snob doesn't mean you should stop. It's important for you to try and make the first attempt and you can always begin by simply smiling and breaking the ice. Conversations are great when they begin with a smile and while you don't have to strike a conversation the very same day you smile at them you could try smiling when you walk past them for a few days before you strike a conversation to make things a little more comfortable.

## Be Kind to Yourself

There would be a lot that goes on daily that will make you feel like you are responsible for certain situations or you could have changed things. You also need to get into the habit of never putting yourself down because it's important for you to understand just how much progress you have made, even if it is a tiny step. There will be mistakes along the way but it's all about reflecting, learning, and rectifying those mistakes as you move on. Sitting and pondering over things that you believe didn't go as planned is not going to help you in any way and the stress will take up your time and may make you feel sad.

While social conventions dictate that you have to be an extrovert in order to be a successful entrepreneur, the truth is that a number of very successful businessmen happen to be introverts. This means there's nothing that can hold you back from achieving the success you want as long as you learn the right method of effective communication when required. The biggest misconception that people have is a person who wants to be a leader needs to be talkative and constantly interact with the people around them but that's not true. If you are an introvert and you want to become successful it's all about effective communication and not the kind of communication that carries on for hours without really being beneficial to anyone.

## Learn About Yourself and Your Skills

One of the most difficult things for a person is to figure out what works for them and whether or not they will manage to use it to their advantage. The most important thing for you to do is to identify your strong points and put it to the best use. While introverts enjoy having a strong conversation, they would prefer to invest their energy into looking for solutions to a problem everyone is focused on rather than talk about it.

## Quality Over Quantity

While introverts prefer to have one-on-one communication or discussions in small groups, they definitely manage to deliver better results because they focus on quality conversations rather than quantity. While an introvert may not have an extremely long meeting and they would not spend too much time discussing with their team, they always make sure they get the message out there and it is done with precision.

## Get Yourself Handy Tools

Introverts manage to use a lot of tools to their advantage and these tools are usually open-ended questions that guarantee them a response from the opposite person. This could be anything from asking them questions about their personal life or even work-related information that can get somebody to talk to you. Sometimes socializing can get the better of you and in such situation is always good to have certain questions ready to ask because this will help you strike a conversation in the most awkward situations and help you relax.

## Invest in Communication

If you've always admired somebody who speaks really well and manages to grab the attention of a lot of people, then you need to start making the effort to become that way. You need to realize that the person you are looking at has invested a lot of time to learn to talk that way. Someone who communicates with you isn't just doing it because it comes to them naturally but it takes a lot of effort for them to do it and you need to do that too. It's not difficult to learn how to communicate effectively. All you need to do is practice it on a regular basis and you will manage to pick up techniques and tips that will help people communicate with you regularly and pay attention to what you have to say.

There is no denying that an introvert requires more time, energy, and effort to become a strong communicator but that does not mean that you can't talk just as well as an extrovert can. All you need to do is take the first step and ask somebody a simple question and you will be able to strike conversations with them on a regular basis. This not only helps to bring out the best of you but it ensures that it keeps your anxiety levels in control even when you can't control the kind of conversations going on around you.

# Chapter 6:
# Leverage Charisma on Command

It is very rare that introverts are considered charismatic. However, there is no reason an introvert cannot build charisma. Once you start developing charisma you will start seeing better things happening around you and the world will look at you as a different person. Some of the advantages of developing your charisma are:

- You will suddenly start finding new friends to go out with at night. People will start inviting you to parties and you will suddenly be part of the fun group.

- If you are a woman, then you will notice guys approaching you more often and asking you to join them for a couple of drinks.

- People will start sharing and opening up with you and they will be eager to strike up a conversation.

Building charisma not only helps build your confidence, it also helps to change your state of mind. Since you will start looking at everything from a positive point of view others will also look at you in the same manner. Here are a few ways that you can develop your charisma and turn your life around.

## Preparing Yourself

Developing charisma requires a little bit of preparation work and it starts even before you leave the house. In order to build charisma, you need to change, physically as well as mentally. In order to connect with people, you need to stop thinking about how tired you will become or how badly you need to get out of a party. When you do not show interest in people you will not receive an interested response back. In order to build charisma, you need to get your mindset right and not allow anything to cause discomfort to you. You need to start being a little warmer and friendlier and focus on what has been handed over to you. To build your charismatic side you will have to start preparing physically and mentally and here are a few ways to get it done:

- Dress for the occasion and be comfortable in your skin.

- Rest a lot so that you do not feel drained while socializing.

- Have a small snack and hydrate yourself well before heading out. Do not overeat because you do not want to feel sick due to indigestion.

- Switch off your work life when you are heading out to socialize as this will help you focus on a single task at hand.

- If you have reached a place where you are extremely uncomfortable then try speaking to your colleagues and change the venue. Do not force yourself to be in an uncomfortable place as this will only ruin your mindset.

## Developing Your Communication Skills

Now that you are physically and mentally prepared you will have to start building on your charm. Although you may be comfortable with your surroundings and with your mindset, you have got to have the right body language and say the right words in order to build on your charisma. How often have you come across a person that looks confident however he or she speaks the wrong words at the wrong time? You can change your clothes and change your mindset time and again however words once spoken cannot be taken back. Here are a few things you need to start controlling in order to start becoming charismatic.

## Your Facial Expressions

You may not realize it but your facial expressions communicate more than the words that come out of your mouth. If you are not comfortable speaking in a group of people then you will have to start controlling your facial expressions as well. You may give out more negative signals than you think and this can put others down. For people that are not very witty and prefer to stay quiet in a group or in a one-on-one conversation, using the right facial expressions is critical. One glance from you can say a lot about your mindset and you need to start controlling this.

## Making Eye Contact

This goes in tandem with your facial expressions. Maintaining eye contact doesn't mean you have to stare into the eyes of the person sitting across you. Your eyes need to have emotion. A blank stare will just end up creeping out the opposite person. If you do not want your eye contact to be awkward, then you have got to have emotions behind it such as:

- Excitement

- Amusement

- Curiosity

- Warmth

- Empathy

While you may feel a lot of negative emotion such as disappointment and anger, try to stay away from such emotions as they will go against your charismatic personality. If you are new to communicating via your eyes then here are a few techniques that you can use to your advantage:

## Imagination

If you want to feel a sense of excitement and you are not getting anything from the conversation you are having with the people around you, try imagining an exciting situation and this will automatically start reflecting in your eyes. Think of the things that excite you such as going on a roller coaster ride or meeting your distant family members after a long time. Once you start imagining these things in your head, your eyes will start reflecting these emotions and the people around you will also see this. Like I said, avoid any negative emotions as this will definitely reflect in your eyes and it will push people further away from you.

## Explore

If you are not very comfortable maintaining eye contact then you can explore the rest of the face. Rather than staring at their eyes you need to notice the other aspects of the face such as the cheeks, the nose and, in the case of a romantic date, even the lips. Although the opposite person will not be able to see you exploring their face, it will help you show your emotions through your eyes when you begin exploring the other aspects of their face. For example, if you notice that your date's lips are very beautiful, it will start showing in your eyes.

## Modulating Your Voice

Modulating your voice and controlling your language are definitely ways to develop charisma. Some women love men with a deep masculine voice while others prefer a man with a thinner voice but better control over language. You also need to take care of how you speak -

women hate being around a man that is too loud and vice-a-versa. You should also control the speed at which you speak. If you speak too fast, the person across you will not understand and if you speak too slowly, they will think you are insulting them. Your voice is also related to your emotion and just like you control your eye contact with your emotions, you can control your voice and your language with the emotions that are playing in your head. You may have seen this with children and with other adults too. If someone is excited about something it will automatically reflect in their voice and you need to keep this in mind when you are communicating with others.

Now let us look at the ways you can build charisma as an introvert. These points can help you develop a personality however there are a few things you should keep in mind as an introvert. These pointers will help you sound confident and build a charismatic personality along with being seductive and charming. The only hindrance for an introvert is their batteries tend to run out very quickly. Let us look at a few points to keep in mind that can help you develop your charisma.

## Be Aware Of Your Limits
Introverts have a limit as far as their energy levels are concerned and you will have to be aware of what your limits are. You cannot go on a wild spree for a couple of days and then take a week to recover from it. Swapping between being an introvert and an extrovert can take a huge toll on your emotions and this can be very difficult to recover from. You should first see how long you can stay at your

energetic best and build from there. Developing a charismatic personality is all about changing your emotional and physical capacity. Rather than pushing your limits on the first day, you have got to make sure that you know your limits first and then work from there.

## Pushing Your Limits

Now that you know what your limits are, you will have to slowly but surely start pushing the limits. You also have to stop short before you start draining out. It is important that you start pushing your limits rather than staying comfortable in your zone. Until you start getting out of your comfort zone you will not be able to develop your charisma.

## Practice Even When No One is Around

There will be times when you are not socializing and you should start practicing your charisma even in your daily life. You could start making a few comments when you go out to have a cup of coffee or even to a restaurant to grab a bite. Start flirting harmlessly with the waitress or try to get a few drinks from the bartender by complimenting him or her. When you start developing your charismatic personality you will get more confident and you will be able to employ these tactics when you socialize. If the above attempts fail, it doesn't matter. These are random people in your life that you would never meet again.

## Start Planning in Advance

**How Quiet Introverts Thrive in An Extrovert World**

You will have to start filtering the events that you attend rather than attending anything and everything that is within sight. You do not have to stress about missing out on a couple of events just because your friends are attending it. Being too social can take a huge toll on your emotional health and you will end up feeling low on energy quite often. Plan your social schedule in advance and slowly build your social momentum.

You also have to remember that building your charisma is not like waving a magic wand. Things are not going to change overnight and you will need to start putting in the right effort in order to improve your social interactions. Right from your personal life to your professional life, you have got to make sure that you display the right body language and say the right things at the right time. The tips mentioned above are just an outline to help you take a step in the right direction. Slowly start by going out with your friends and see how comfortable you are while mingling in a social environment. If you love what you feel then you will be more confident while building your charisma.

# Chapter 7:
# Tips for Networking and Making Friends

Making friends may seem difficult for introverts because they often shy away from people and do not open up to them as easily as an extrovert would. That doesn't mean that introverts can't make friends and while you always stay close to the people you know all your life, there's no harm in exploring a little further and getting to know new people. Although socializing is something that doesn't come naturally to an introvert, it doesn't mean that you can never learn how to make new friends. If you have shifted to a new city or a town and you are finding it difficult to adjust because there is nobody you really know, then you have to make a little effort to get to know people and start living a social life.

If you want to socialize in a new place it's important to have somebody to go with. While making that friend could be a little difficult at the start, with a little effort you will be able to make new friends and learn how to stay close. If you are wondering what you should do to make new friends and increase your circle of friends here are some things that can help you.

## Think About People You Already Know

The best way to expand your social circle and get to know people a little better is to begin with acquaintances or people who you see on a regular basis. If you head to a coffee shop every morning to grab your cup of coffee and you notice somebody is sitting there reading a newspaper or with a laptop, begin by exchanging pleasantries with them. The reason it is always better to begin with people you see on a regular basis or the people you acknowledge, is because you will start to feel more comfortable with them. Write down a list of people that could potentially be your friends and while this may sound weird; it's a great way to begin a friendship with someone who you will be able to select rather than randomly talking to somebody just because you felt like it. When you shift to a new city it is very likely that you feel left out because there is nobody to talk to. Unless you begin to look for people who you can call your friends you will always feel this way.

Whether it is at your workplace or outside of work, there will always be people who you see, and be able to socialize with regularly. These are the kind of people that could be there for you. Even when you are at work try to look for someone who lives close to your house so you get to spend more time with the person. Introverts need time to open up and for this reason, you may want to look for someone who can spend time with you at work and outside of work, if possible. The reason it is important to look for someone who lives close to you or works with you is because it is that much easier to schedule meetings with them in comparison to doing it with someone who lives out of your locality or works at a different schedule from you. Even if you find somebody who doesn't work with you, try to ensure they have a similar schedule so you will be able to socialize a lot.

## You May Have to Make the First Move

You will spot a lot of people who you may believe are potential friends for you but they might not approach you. This means that you are left with no option but to go ahead and make the first move. While you are an introvert there is also a chance the person you may want to go and begin a conversation with is also an introvert and they may not have the courage to approach you to start the conversation. Whether you want to speak to somebody you want to be friends with or someone that you would like to get romantically involved with, it is important for you to understand that making the first move is not wrong and in fact it gives you the upper hand in deciding which people you want to talk to and which ones you may not want to be friends with.

Making the first move can be really difficult but it is a lot easier than you think, especially when there's no other option. You can always begin with small talk and analyze the person to decide whether or not you will manage to get along with them. While you won't have to put in too much effort to make friends with somebody, it will take you a little while to understand whether or not you can be friends with someone who approached you depending on the kind of lifestyle they lead. If they are extremely social and they love going out on a regular basis, you may not be able to keep up with them because socializing is one of your weaknesses. While you may manage to incorporate socialization for a couple of times in your routine, it may not be something you look forward to doing on a regular basis. Looking for somebody who has similar interests as you always work out well, so if you enjoy reading you may want to hang out at the library to see similar faces you can interact with.

**Taking off the Mask**
One of the biggest mistakes an introvert makes is to try and behave like somebody they are not. The truth is that while it may seem like a great idea at the start because it will help you make many friends, it's not an ideal solution because you will eventually get bored of portraying an image you are not. This also makes it difficult for you to live up to the expectations of your new friend.

Honesty is always the best policy and even if you like somebody but you do not share similar interests, it's better to be honest and figure out how to work out your differences rather than pretend to like what they like, just to get in their good books.

Introverts are often labeled as submissive people who give in to the needs of others; the truth, however, is very different from that. If you don't like something, you'll eventually figure out excuses to get out of the situation and that won't benefit your friendship in any way. It makes more sense for you to let people know your true personality, beliefs, likes and dislikes rather than asking them to like you by pretending to do something just because they like it.

It may take you a while to find people who get along with you, who understand your needs, and your likes and dislikes, but it doesn't make sense to make friends with someone just because you do not like being alone. One of the strong points of an introvert is that they manage to analyze people really well and this can work out in your favor when you look out for somebody to make friends with or even start a romantic relationship with.

**Questions Are Good**

If you want to make friends with someone, it is important for you to start questioning them. While this may sound like an unreasonable thing to do, once you begin questioning, you will realize that you get to know more about them than you ever thought possible. This will also help you to get closer to them. Whether you want to get close to somebody at your workplace or outside of your workplace the more you question them the more you learn about them. This will help you to connect more effectively with the person you are in conversation with.

There are various people you will be surrounded by and once you've narrowed down the people you think you should get close to; you should try to talk to them at every possible opportunity so you can get to know them a little better. You don't have to have a detailed conversation but simple questions about how they are doing or their personal life is something that will definitely grab their interest and you will also manage to strike conversations with them easily. Your listening skills are definitely your strength when it comes to questioning. When you ask somebody a question you always make it a point to put all your efforts into listening to what they have to say because every little detail matter to you. This not only helps you to use their information as a conversation starter later on, but it also lets them know that you are actually interested in getting to know them and this helps your friendship take another step closer.

**Pay Attention to Your Feelings**

Introverts often get confused with regards to whether or not they should become friends with a particular person. It may take you a while to understand your compatibility with somebody and in case you find it difficult to know your feelings at the start, take a little time to analyze the situation.

Your feelings towards the person matter a lot and whether or not you are actually happy to see the person is something you need to consider before making friends with them. When you look at someone and it makes you feel like going and approaching them to talk, this is a good sign. It means that you want to be friends with them, not just because you are lonely, but because you believe that they are good people. Take time to see how you feel when you see someone or plan to briefly interact with them before you actually have a longer interaction, because this may help you understand how effectively you will be able to bond with them. Subconsciously, introverts make an extra effort to bond with people they actually like. So, try to look for these people before you begin your friend hunt.

It's the same with somebody that you want to get romantically involved with. In case you are being set up on a date with someone, see how you feel about the date once you meet them and whether or not meeting them for a second time makes you feel happy or anxious. As an introvert, the one thing you should always pay attention to is meeting someone who is as comfortable as you are in a conversation and makes you feel happy rather than stressed out about discussing a topic. While there are a number of people who can make it very easy for an introvert to talk to them, there are some that are little difficult to get through and these are the kind of people you may want to stay away from, especially if you are approaching them alone.

### The Awkwardness Eventually Goes Away
One of the biggest problems of being an introvert is the awkward feeling you have every time you walk close to someone to greet them or even to exchange pleasantries. It's funny how this feeling is extremely strong at the start but once you repeat the habit over and over again, you notice that it goes away.

It's the same with every new person you see. For the first time, you may have a little choking sensation in your throat and you may not want to talk to them or even let your eyes meet theirs, but once you start talking you will realize that it's not that bad and you are getting comfortable around them. Some people are easier to get along with and others may take a longer time, so don't give up on the first instance - just push a little harder. At the end of the day, you won't lose too much if exchanging pleasantries is all that you are stuck on. The good news is you don't have to have a full conversation with them but you can still manage to get a little comfortable when compared to what you were at the start.

There are going to be a lot of people who work around you and you can't expect to get along with all of them. You have to pick the people you hang out with. Pick the kind of people you know you will be yourself around. This may not happen instantly. Sometimes it may take weeks and even months but when you do find your clan, you will start adjusting a lot better, whether it's your workplace or a new place that you settled in.

### Schedule Meetings Regularly

Everyone is busy these days and leading a hectic life has become one of the most common excuses to get away from social situations. If you keep on delaying a social interaction with people you just met, you will not manage to blossom the friendship or even a relationship that you plan on starting out.

As difficult as it sounds, you have to schedule regular interactions or meetings with them. This could be anything as simple as catching a movie where you don't really have to talk to them for a long time. Meeting them over a couple of drinks to get to know them better is also perfectly acceptable.

It is a little scary to do this but it's something that will help you come out and become more confident. The reason you should always try and interact with people as much as possible is to you learn more about them and to learn whether or not you can get closer to them as a friend or whether you just want to have them as one of those people you know. Introverts need a lot of time to open up to someone and the more you spend time with them, the easier it will get for you to do this. When you make friends, make sure that you make the most of it and try going out as often as possible to let the awkwardness out of your life completely.

## Go Slow

Introverts always fear that they will get hurt if their friendship doesn't work out the way they wanted it to or a romantic relationship does not turn out to be a good relationship. All good things take time and that's the same for genuine, strong friendship or relationship. So, you have to make sure you invest that time whenever possible.

You also need to remember that just because there are a few differences between you and your friend doesn't mean you give up.

**How Quiet Introverts Thrive in An Extrovert World**

Everyone has to make a little adjustment and you are not going to like everything about a person. So, give them a fair chance once you get to know them a little better and let them get to know more about you too. Once you start spending time with them you will learn a lot more about them and you never know which way it could go. If you decide after few months that you are not happy hanging out with these people, you can always look for a new friend to hang out with. But if it works out in your favor, you would have found yourself a group of people you can actually call your own and the kind of people who understand you for who you truly are.

# Chapter 8:
# Survival Guide for Social Events

No matter how hard you try to come out of your shell, there are certain limits for every introvert. Social gatherings are always a stressful matter and while introverts make an effort to go to social gatherings, they believe are important, they often look for ways to escape. While it is good to make excuses every now and then if you're overdoing your social interaction, you also need to make sure that you involve yourself in socializing as much as possible so that you get to know more people, moving out of your comfort zone a little every time. If you are a loner and you have never gone out for social gatherings then this social survival guide can help you get through the scariest of social gatherings without any problems. It is something that you should keep handy so you can use it to your advantage.

**Find a Quiet Spot**
There is no denying that introverts tend to look for the quietest spots and go park themselves in those spots for the rest of the evening. It's not easy to find a spot every time because sometimes you go to a gathering at a new place and you are not really sure about the venue. If you are hosting a party then you know exactly where the quiet spot

is but you may not be able to get to the spot as conveniently as possible. This is because you have to stay the center of attraction and constantly greet guests when they walk through the door.

If you are visiting somebody's house, look for a quiet spot in one of the corners where not a lot of people are gathering around. A trick to find these corners would be to look for places that are as far away from the bar as possible because the bar is where all the extroverts and the talkative people will usually gather. Once you find your safe place you can then get comfortable and maybe look for someone to talk to. Introverts prefer to talk to one person, or probably two or three people, at a time. Try to look for these people and try to gel with them for the rest of the party. If it's an outdoor event then you may want to look for places such as the corners of the venue that are not too close to the door because people will keep coming in and leaving. If it's a house party then bedrooms, bathrooms, corridors, and the kitchen are great places to hangout. If the bedroom door is shut, you may want to stay out of it because you have absolutely no clue what's going on inside and you do not want to be the person to witness it.

If it is a restaurant where you are meeting then you can always take the corner seat at the table so you don't have to be in between a lot of people. If you want to make sure that you get the corner seat you may want to arrive at the restaurant a little earlier than the rest of the crowd.

## Keep A Check on Your Energy Levels

Socializing can get your anxiety levels right to the top and it could become difficult for you to constantly interact with people by staying in a pleasant mood. The best way to keep yourself calm and composed during these interactions is to talk to people for a little while and then focus on what you are eating or maybe even pull out your phone to distract yourself from the conversation. There are going to be constant outbursts of high-energy where you feel comfortable as a part of the group and are constantly discussing things with them without realizing that you were awkward in the first place. There will also be moments where you want everyone at the table to just be quiet so you can relax for a while.

The minute you start feeling a little anxious you can always excuse yourself and go to the bathroom until you calm down your nerves. Sometimes you just feel a little overwhelmed by the conversations that are going on around you and because you don't want to be mean, you try to make an effort to talk but that does not help. This is normal for an introvert and when you start feeling this way just give yourself a little 'me time' away from the crowd so you can get back into your high energy zone.

Sometimes it can take you a little longer to get back to your original high-energy zone so you can always let people know that you are not feeling too well, which is why you aren't talking. This helps you to relax for a while and it gives you a fair chance to listen to what is happening around the table. When you know the conversations around the table, it gets easier for you to jump in whenever you feel comfortable or when the conversation starts to interest you. This is a great way to face your fears and deal with it at the same time without letting your anxiety get the better of you.

## Go with Someone

If you are really nervous about attending a party alone, look for someone you can go with. The person that you plan on going with should always be somebody that you trust and you are close to so that you can plan an escape whenever possible. While introverts can make a lot of effort to attend parties and also make it a point to talk to people, they don't know that well, large gatherings make them feel uncomfortable and the only thing they want to do is head home and stay away from the crowd.

If you have made an effort to get to a party with your friend, it's a great achievement on your end and there's nothing to feel embarrassed about in case you are not feeling like staying for the rest of the evening. The reason it is always recommended to have somebody by your side is because leaving a party alone can make you feel upset and sad and it will also make you feel like you have no friends. When you have someone by your side you don't tend to feel so bad about it and you can even choose to go and head out for a dinner or even grab a couple of drinks a little later on.

Friends are the kind of people you feel comfortable with and if you do not go with someone then you will have a low energy level even after the event. However, taking somebody with you will help increase your energy as soon as you are out of an uncomfortable situation. It also ensures that you've done something productive rather than getting home and talking about not being able to participate in socializing. You need to remember that whether you are out with one person or you are out with a ton of people, it is still considered socializing so don't beat yourself up just because you had a bad day or you couldn't get along with the people at the party.

## Plan Your Leaving Time

One of the worst things that an introvert contemplates is when they can leave a party the minute, they step in. Instead of doing this, have a clear plan in your head from the start and tell yourself that you are not going to leave the party any sooner than a particular time or any later than that. While staying a little later is definitely a good sign, leaving earlier is something that you should prevent yourself from doing.

If you absolutely dread the party, you need to remind yourself that you only have a couple of hours more to stay till you can escape for the night. During this time, rather than focusing on how much time is left before you leave, try to interact with people and do something to help kill the time. This is another reason it is highly recommended to go with a friend; because you can always strike a conversation with your friend at the party and talk about the things you like. Not only will that help you to relax, it will even help you to take your mind off your agenda of leaving the party early.

You never know, you may end up finding a bunch of people who interest you, make you feel comfortable even though you just met them, and make you feel like these are the kind of people you would want to spend more time with. Just because you set a certain time to leave the party doesn't mean you have to leave it at that time. If you're having a good time, try staying for as long as you can but make sure that you are safe and you always have somebody with you that you've known for a long time.

As an introvert you should also make sure that you have a lot of independence which means you should have rideshared applications on your phone or even the number of a cab driver you trust who will be available all the time and can come and get you wherever you are.

### Make Sure You Know the Guest List

This may seem irrelevant because you can't really control who attends and doesn't attend the party but the reason it is better for you to know the kind of people on the list is because you know exactly how comfortable you will be right from the start. If there are a bunch of people you usually enjoy spending time with on the list, you know that you would be able to enjoy the party but if there are a number of people on the list that you find awkward to talk to, then you can plan your escape or even consider skipping the party.

Just because you are making an effort to socialize doesn't necessarily mean you have to attend every single party you are invited to because then it will be pushing yourself to a limit that's not healthy and comfortable. You need to balance your life in a way where you attend a certain number of social events that you actually enjoy and avoid the ones you know you are going to have a bad time at. This is not going to happen instantly and you may end up attending some really bad parties and miss out on some really good ones. However, with a little trial and error you will be able to figure out which are the ones you should go to and which are the ones you should sit out. Knowing the guest list is a great way to decide which one you should attend and which one you should sit out because the kind of people that attend the party is the only thing that is important, rather than what kind of food was served or what was the venue of the party.

## Listen Attentively and Talk Less

When you are an introvert at a party, listen attentively to everything the people are saying and talk as little as possible. This benefits you in a number of ways because when someone speaks to you and asks you something, you know what to say to them because you have been paying attention to the conversation.

This doesn't necessarily mean that you stop talking completely. It just means that you listen to other people a little more than you talk. You will come across a lot of self-centered people who love talking about themselves and how great they are and this may bore you completely. In such situations the best thing to do would be to move away from these people and focus on a group of people you actually think you will be able to blend in with.

You do not need to be apologetic for not liking somebody or not being able to get along with them. You have your choices to make and at the end of the day every party is for you to feel good and not embarrass you or make you feel awkward in anyway. The minute you realize you are in an uncomfortable situation you should try and move towards a situation or a group of people that make you feel more comfortable because that's when you will start liking social gatherings rather than dreading them. Instead of forcing yourself to do something you do not like, find something you like at social gatherings because that's what really matters.

### Take Up A Helping Role

One of the smartest ways to be a part of a social gathering without actually involving yourself in an active conversation is by lending a helping hand to the host. This could be anything such as cutting of the cake and making it into smaller pieces that people can eat or even trying to arrange the salad on a plate.

This works really well because you start blending with people in a certain manner and this is what works in your favor. Instead of pushing your boundaries, you may want to do something you are comfortable with.

At the end of the day every introvert is different from another and you have to find your comfortable space at social gatherings to make yourself like the gathering. You cannot push yourself to do something you don't like because that would be trying to become a person you are not. Find a reason to enjoy this party rather than looking for ways to do it because that will help you a lot better.

# Chapter 9:
# Outsell the Extroverts

Just because you are an introvert doesn't mean you won't be able to do well in life or you will not be good at what you do. As I stated before, most introverts tend to be highly successful as long as they know how to use their strength to their advantage.

Just because you may struggle to proactively stand up and talk to somebody doesn't mean that you are not going to form healthy relationships with people. As long as you know when to say things to people, not only will you be able to achieve success but there is a chance that you will do better than an extrovert ever will. Let's look at some effective ways with regards to how you can use your strength to gain success and give yourself an equal chance to stand out in front of your peers.

### Be Consistent
One of the major lessons you have got to learn in life is to maintain consistency at what you do. While you have to strive to get better every day you have to make sure that you do not step backward in the race. You should keep motivating yourself to get better and

improve your skill sets so that you can deliver great results. You will not have to be a part of a lengthy discussion in order to deliver better results. However, what you should do is to make sure your work speaks for itself. There is no denying that actions do speak louder than words and this is where your actions will come into play.

You will have to communicate with people to ensure the message is clearly passed on and everybody who is part of the team understands the job correctly. However, pondering over the same discussion for a long time is not going to benefit you because that way all you will do is waste time talking rather than doing something for the organization. Communication should always be short, precise, and consistent so that your team knows exactly what sort of questions they have to ask you in order to flawlessly complete the task on time. Swift communication is definitely better and this helps you to be more consistent without complicating matters.

### Focus on Your Goal

Whether you are leading a team or whether you are part of it, your main aim should be to focus on the goal and achieve it in the best possible manner rather than seeing what all the people are doing. If you are a leader you need to pay attention to what others are doing so that you can direct them in the right path but it does not mean that you hover over them and tell them how they should do their work. Everybody has their own way of working and the reason an introvert is better able to deal with the situations is because they do not like to interfere with the working style of a person and they give them their space.

At the end of the day your main goal should be delivering effective, consistent, and reliable results rather than seeing how your team works on it. When you try to correct them too many times it won't work out in your favor because you will constantly interfere with the workflow and this will de-motivate them. The reason an introvert needs to learn to push the buttons of their team members a little bit is because they sometimes tend to get overheard and nobody pays attention to what they are saying.

While you should not force your team members to work in a particular style you should always give them a path that you believe is strong. Whether or not they choose to walk on that path is completely left up to them, as long as they deliver the result in the manner you have requested. This is where your consistency, systematic and effective practice comes into play. It helps them become better and eventually not only will you be strong and goal oriented but you have a team of strong headed and goal-oriented members working with you.

## Take Calculated Risks

Introverts don't like to step outside of their comfort zone and this also includes the fact that they do not like to take risks because they believe it will not work out in their favor. If you are certain that something can be done better with a little risk involved then you should consider trying out the new techniques to see where it goes.

Success and failure are all part of the plan and you cannot expect everything to go your way all the time and move ahead in life. There are going to be times when you are challenged with questions you may not be comfortable answering and decisions you may not be comfortable taking. However, it's all about how you approach the situation and what you do under the circumstances that let you know whether or not you are doing the right thing. Take your time to calculate the risks involved and see whether or not it actually pays off so that you can decide how to spruce up your game.

Another smart thing for you to decide whether or not taking risks makes sense is to observe what your competition is up to. Admiring their techniques and seeing how certain strategies worked out for them is something that can help you come up a strategic plan. It doesn't take you too long to learn new things and neither will it take your team to do so. All you have to do is understand whether or not the decision you want to take will work out in the benefit of your business or not.

### Learn New Technology

Learning new technology is something that will accelerate your growth, not only professionally but also personally. It is something that can help you to learn to develop new skills and if you someday dream of becoming an entrepreneur, it is these technological advancements that can help you take that step ahead. Becoming a leader is important and in order for you to do this, embracing new technology is something that you may want to consider doing. It helps you to get a competitive edge and it helps you to learn the market in a smarter way.

You will not be able to try out new technology unless you are open to taking calculated risks which is why you need to first learn how to do that properly. While it is important for you to learn certain business strategies by working for someone, your end goal should always be to start a business of your own that you can handle from scratch and you will only be able to do this once you increase your knowledge. In order for you to increase your knowledge you have to be open to change and taking risks that you were uncomfortable taking in the past. You have to learn how to challenge yourself if you want to grow because if you do not challenge yourself to do something new, you cannot get different results by doing the same thing over and over again.

## Analyze Your Business

One of the most important things that you need to do is to analyze your business so that you are able to identify every little mistake that is made and come up with solutions before other people. Introverts are always at a benefit because they spend a lot of time analyzing situations and paying attention to every little detail that is discussed.

You should always use this to your advantage and make note of the important things that you listen to from time to time. This is information that you can definitely use to your benefit and make the most out of. Once you get this sort of information sorted out you will manage to invest in your own business ideas in the future.

Nothing is irrelevant and the more information you gather the stronger your business will grow which is why you should start paying attention to every little thing that you hear around you, even if it does not relate to your area of interest.

Just because you are an introvert does not mean that you cannot become a successful businessman someday. You need to start building your strong foundation from today and it all begins by taking the right decisions. Small changes in your life can make a huge impact in the future so begin making the changes today so that you become a creature of habit to do the right thing at the right time.

Once you gave laid the foundation towards learning effective tips on how you can become a successful entrepreneur you then need to put these tips into action.

It is common for an introvert to feel overwhelmed when they start something as big as their own venture but with a little practice and the right measures not only will you manage to make this a successful business but you'll also manage to grow and achieve your goal that you set out to achieve.

## How Quiet Introverts Thrive in An Extrovert World

Introverts make amazing entrepreneurs because they are smart, self-aware and they invest a lot of time in research which is vital for the growth and success of any business. Since they do not invest a lot of their time in discussion, they have that much more time to invest in the actual business and this helps them to maximize their revenue by enhancing their skills and exploiting the talent to the fullest. There are various reasons why introverts can be successful entrepreneurs but if you are still a little worried with regards to how you should actually go about setting up your own business here are a few strategies that you could definitely apply.

### Maximize Your Leadership Potential

An introvert usually spends time researching the best possible business practices that they believe will work well in their favor. However, a particular business strategy will not necessarily work as effectively for your business as it did for another business. If you want to truly become successful and grow your business the smart thing for you to do would be to spend time understanding what everyone around you has to say. Introverts are more likely to take advice from people rather than make their own decisions, so when you ask a team of employees for suggestions and ways to spruce up the business, you are more likely to come up with a foolproof business plan that will not only increase productivity amongst the employees but also help the business grow more effectively. The best part about a business growing like this is you have a team of highly motivated employees who have given inputs towards the business which make them feel proud about every achievement the business makes.

## Consider Hiring an Extroverted Partner

There is no shame in admitting that there are certain skills an extrovert possesses that an introvert does not and it makes sense to have a charismatic character in the business for betterment and growth. There is a high chance that an introvert has many extrovert friends and for you to be able to comfortably include someone in the business, it always makes sense to look at someone who's been around with you for a long time.

If we look at history, then the most prominent businesses usually started off with an introvert-extrovert pairing. Once you find someone you can actually set your rhythm with, it makes sense to include them in the business because they come with their own skill sets and those skills can definitely help a business grow in leaps and bounds. When it comes to handling meetings and taking certain decisions an extrovert will always step up and prove to be a valuable asset.

## Schedule One-on-One Meetings

Introverts often have a problem with large groups and when you have to talk to a room full of people you might not be able to get your message across as effectively because your anxiety levels will automatically start increasing. The smarter way for you to deal with the situation would be to have a one-on-one meeting with people you believe can work well for you. The reason this is important is because this meeting not only turns out to be more productive but you also manage to convey your side of the story to your employer and you can let them know what you are looking for. Another way to go about this is to hire a manager that can handle the handling of the team for you. You will be able to conduct one-on-one meeting with them; they can take charge on their own and make sure that they get the message passed down to the rest of the team. While one-on-one meetings are highly beneficial it can't be done when you have multiple employees because that will take up a huge amount of your time. When you have a manager to handle all of this for you, all you need to do is to get the message to your manager effectively and they can then take charge.

## Self-Promote

Self-promotion can be difficult for an introvert because they don't find it easy to strike a conversation in front of people. However, considering today's technologically savvy industry, one can now share their story by simply writing it down and putting it on social media or on a blog for the world to see. This is a lot of fun and it also helps you to let people know what your business is all about and how effective it actually is. The suggestions you get on your social media page can not only help you feel more confident but it also helps you to bring about the change that is necessary to spruce up your business. Most introverts are amazing writers so you may want to give this a try.

**Samuel C. Larson**

If you are adamant about establishing your own business, the one thing you should always make sure is that you got it all covered and you take your decisions one step at a time when jumping into a completely new venture. As exciting as it may sound, introverts need to do their homework properly so that they can carry out the business operations successfully.

# Chapter 10:
# Crush Your Competitors

Introverts find it a little difficult to deal with competition in comparison to extroverts but that does not mean that they should give into the pressure and succumb. If you've gone as far as to establish your own business and decided to become an entrepreneur nothing will stop you from being successful as long as you learn how to beat your competition effectively. Just because someone is outgoing and charismatic, it does not take away your own charm and while they have skill sets of their own, you possess your own unique skill sets that can make you stand out and shine.

According to Forbes about 50% of the US population happens to be introverts so you are not alone out there. About half the population in your country is exactly the way you are. Although there are different levels of introversion, they are normally disregarded. They're also often passed off as submissive people who can't make decisions. The truth however is that an introvert doesn't necessarily have to be an outgoing person and while they may enjoy going out and having a good time, they just like to do it with a chosen few people because they are not comfortable with a large crowd.

Introverts can make amazing business leaders, just like extroverts, and when it comes to crushing competition they are not far behind. If anything, introverts can give extroverts a run for their money because of their intuitive behavior and listening skills. If you are wondering how an introvert can push the limits and become successful to beat competition then here are a few things you should know about yourself.

**You'll Make a Great Leader**
Introverts often believe that they cannot handle a business because they can't face a large crowd and this means that they can't lead a group. The truth, however, is that an introvert is just as effective as an extrovert when it comes to running a business and while they may not be able to look into the eyes of a large group of people for a meeting, they will still be able to be effective. A number of large businessmen today happen to be introverts so there is nothing that can stop you from achieving your dream as long as you have a plan in place. The reason an introvert has a strong chance of becoming successful is because they take calculated risks and they invest sufficient time in research which helps them to understand the market they are venturing into before they get into it. An introvert will not make an immediate decision but rather spend time understanding whether or not it is worth taking before they actually decide on it and this means that the risk of losing money is drastically reduced. Extroverts on the other hand end up making impulse decisions they later regret which

is why the chances of them becoming successful entrepreneurs is actually lower than an introvert.

An introvert masters many skills when it comes to growing a business and these skills turn out to be the reason an introvert is also known to be great at relationships, personally and professionally.

- Reliable
- Dependable
- Adaptable

Although a number of people believe that it is difficult for an introvert to adapt to new situations the truth is, they know to do it better and with ease in comparison to an extrovert. If you want to crush your competition then here are a few things you should remember

**Focus on Your Strength**
It is easy for an introvert to get excited about business ideas they are passionate about, but they also get really scared once they have actually taken the step into it. Once you have decided you want to become an entrepreneur you should aim to be a successful one and this means that you need to start making the most of your strengths. Even though you may not enjoy talking so much, you will definitely enjoy researching, writing, and even mentoring so try to figure out what works best for you and put that to your advantage. The minute you

start paying attention to your strengths, you will learn how to use it to better your business, which will help your business to grow leaps and bounds.

## Modify Your Weakness

If you know that you are not good at something then always try to get somebody to get the task completed for you. This could be anybody from a business partner to an employee you trust. Everyone comes with their flaws and it's the same for an introvert, so there's nothing to be ashamed of when it comes to lacking in a particular area of skill or expertise. If there is something that you cannot do or you do not understand, asking questions is not a shame even if you are at the highest position.

## Hiring a Business Partner

The reason it is important to try and look for an extrovert is because you will always compliment and balance the skill set perfectly. A partnership that is in the form of an extrovert-introvert partnership turns out to be the smartest and the most successful partnership because this partnership will be highly skilled. It also helps you to cover up your flaws and it works the same way for your partner as well.

## Recharge Yourself

No matter how far you come with your life an introvert will always need a little more time which allows them to relax and go back to everything that happened during the course of the day. The reason this is something you should not let go of is because it helps you to reflect upon the various things you did and this helps you figure out where you went wrong, in case something did not go your way. When you let yourself relax and look back upon what you did during the course of the day, it helps you to better your actions for the following days and also make better decisions in the future.

## Rejuvenate

Another important task that you should always focus on doing, no matter how busy you are, is to rejuvenate. Whatever you like to do, you should make time to do. This could include walking a nature trail or simply spending time in bed thinking about your next move. If you like visiting the salon and getting a massage alone do it because this is something that will help you feel fresh and geared up for the next hectic day at work.

When it comes to beating competition, you can't do it instantly. You need to have a strategic plan in place. Begin working on your plan from day one and continue working on it for the rest of your life. When you beat competition today, they going to try and get back at you so you should ensure you don't let them reach you once you have overtaken them. This requires a lot of work and planning.

Now that we have established that introverts can become successful entrepreneurs it's important to figure out strategies that can help introverts market their business effectively. While it is easy to handle your business with a strong team, marketing is something you might not be really good at because this is when you have to face the audience and talk to people you don't really know that well. As an introvert you will manage to handle every other aspect of your business confidently but when it comes to dealing with people that you are not familiar with, things could get a little difficult. Let's take a look at some effective strategies you can apply to your marketing strategies for your business.

## Use Low Introduction Marketing Techniques

While face-to-face marketing may be something you are not confident with, you can always explore various other methods of marketing that can use your strength to your benefit. These days there are a number of marketing techniques that work out really well and this includes online marketing which does not involve any sort of interaction. The best part of online marketing is that it helps you to touch base with a ton of people without having to worry about personally interacting with them. This is one of the best ways to market your business especially when you are an introvert.

Sending out emails is also a smart technique of marketing if you are involved in a B2B (business-to-business) scenario because you will need to start a conversation with unknown businesses or people that you've never met before. Emails are a great way to break the ice and begin a conversation without any awkwardness. Design a few email

### How Quiet Introverts Thrive in An Extrovert World

templates to use for the emails you send out and you can choose between them whenever required. This can help you to build rapport with the person before you actually pick up the phone and give them a call or schedule a meeting with them. If you are still not very confident meeting somebody face-to-face then you can always send in your marketing representative to do the rest of the job.

Podcasting is another way for your business to stay at the top of its competitive edge without you having to face the crowd, literally. Everybody wants to hear from the entrepreneur at least once and this is the reason why podcasting is highly beneficial. It helps people know what you are thinking and you can confidently discuss the matter by simply recording whatever it is that you want to portray. Podcasts are a great way to make you famous without having to step up on a stage and discuss with people.

Blogging and guest posting also works just as effectively because it helps you to explain your business in your own words. Introverts are really creative and they can come up with articles to share with potential clients that can help grab attention.

Regular social media marketing and other techniques also help you to market your business without getting out there in the open. This helps you to feel confident and it ensures that your business grows without having to step outside of your comfort zone.

One of the best things about being an introvert is that you have a ton of skills. Extroverts may not possess these skills and this includes spending a lot of time in listening to what other people have to say and researching about material that you can share with others.

When you send out emails or create videos or talking to an audience, you can always address all of these problems and ensure that you get all questions answered. Introverts have amazing problem-solving skills and this makes them stand out amongst the crowd when it comes to offering advice. While you may not be great at the traditional marketing methods, this is where you'll actually shine and you will not only manage to let people know how skillful and knowledgeable you are but it will also help in establishing a strong relationship that matters. One of the best things about introverts is that they do not use marketing gimmicks to promote products and they try to be as authentic and real as possible.

Once you learn how to use your skill set to your advantage not only will you manage to crush your competition but you will manage to stay at the top for a really long time. Not only do introverts manage to grow their business fast but they also manage to establish a brand name that stays in the market for a long time thereby ensuring that their business adds value to customers.

# Chapter 11:
# Make Yourself Known

All said and done, one of the most difficult things for any introvert is to start executing a lot of confidence in themselves. While it is difficult to feel confident when you are not comfortable talking to strangers or a large crowd, this is something you will have to learn to do on your own - one step at a time. There are a number of decisions you need to make in order to feel confident but it will not come to you instantly. It requires a lot of hard work and effort from your end but once you do make an effort, it will eventually pay off. You need to remember that just because you can't talk to many people confidently doesn't make you a shy person or a bad person. However, if you want to improve your skills and learn how to approach a large crowd without feeling anxious then these confidence tips will help you get there.

**You May Need to Pretend A Little**
An introvert needs to learn how to socialize with people and there is no denying that they can't do it instantly because they are not confident enough to get it done at the first try. However, if you want to feel confident about yourself then a smart thing would be to approach the situation in a systematic and effective way. You need to start

pretending that you actually enjoying socializing and talking to people even though you don't know who they are. The reason it's important for you to try and pretend is because this helps you to cover up the anxiety that you begin to feel the minute you come across a situation you are not comfortable with.

Pretending may sound fake and this is something you may want to avoid but honestly, it's the best method to practice being confident when you are actually not. It helps you to work with your head held high and it makes you feel a lot better about yourself. The reason you should try pretending to enjoy certain situations is because pretending over and over again will eventually make you actually enjoy the situation and you won't even realize when that changed. In order for you to pretend, you need to make sure that you don't push yourself too much because that's when things will get out of hand and you will eventually give up. Start with little changes and pretend to enjoy them bit by bit till you actually start liking them. Introduce these changes one step at a time.

## Stay Close to People You Know

Irrespective of what you do in life or how successful you become; your close friends will always be the most important people to you. These are the kind of people you will feel comfortable with and spending time with them will help increase your confidence levels tremendously. When you start feeling confident with a small group of people, that's when you eventually start getting more comfortable with larger crowds. If you want to try out something new, it is safest to try it out with your own group of people because you know that they will never judge you and never say anything bad about your behavior. One of the biggest fears that introverts have is that someone will make fun of them and that's the reason why they stay quiet. When you start experimenting with your friends, they will be honest with you and tell you in a very nice way whether or not it works. This helps you to try out things that work in front of people you do not know that well and when they appreciate your actions your confidence level starts to increase.

It is also important for you to be in a relationship that is not toxic and filled with negative energy. You should always try to surround yourself with people who fill your life with positivity and eliminate the negativity from your life rather than introducing it into your daily routine. If somebody keeps telling you that you cannot do something, try avoiding these people completely because they are bad for your confidence level.

### Give Yourself Alone Time that Counts

It is important for every introvert to spend some time alone, without socializing, in order to reflect on what has happened in their life. However, when you do take a break from the world you need to do something positive with it, like reading a book or watching a movie that is educational and informative. The time you spend with yourself should not be reflected upon feeling bad for yourself or making decisions that will make you feel sad. Rather it should be something that can help you boost your confidence levels by relaxing. Watching a comedy is something that's really important because laughter is the best medicine for almost everything and it's a great way to feel more confident about yourself.

Once you start releasing a lot of positive energy you automatically reduce your stress levels and when this happens, you feel better about who you are. Lowering your stress levels is important and while you may not be able to do this in front of a group of people, you will manage to do this when you are by yourself and it is important that you do this regularly. Even if it means trying to get home a little early from work just so that you could spend time rejuvenating by soaking your feet in warm water and essential oils - Do it! Soothing music is also known to work wonders to relieve stress and help you feel good about yourself. If you had a hectic day at work and someone has said something to lower your morale, all you need to do is give yourself some 'me time' and do something positive with it so you can come back with a bang and be more confident than ever.

## Dress Your Best

This may sound redundant right now but it is very important for you to dress well and dress in a manner that you are confident. You shouldn't be wearing something because everyone is wearing it. You should do it because you are happy when you wear it. Dressing up is an excellent way to boost your confidence and it will help you to feel good about yourself. Every month make sure to set aside a certain amount of money to invest in good clothes, accessories and shoes that you can flaunt.

Not only are clothes and accessories an amazing conversation starter but they will make you feel good. When dressing up, you have to ensure you wear clothes that are stylish and classy. Always ask yourself how you feel once you are wearing a particular outfit and make sure that that's the way you want to present yourself in front of a large crowd. When choosing the right kind of clothes try to invest in quality over quantity because good clothes speak volumes about you and make you feel a lot better about who you are. A good tailor-made outfit can also help you cover up your flaws which happens to be a downer for a number of introverts.

## Stop Comparing

If you want to become a confident person the first step that you should take is to stop comparing yourself to others. Your individuality lies in who you are and not what you can compare with others. You have got to learn how to be comfortable in your own skin and appreciate your own skill sets rather than looking at what another person has done and try to copy them just because you think they are better than you. If you want to become a confident person the first thing that you have to tell yourself is that you are unique, there is no one like you, and you are the only competition you have to face.

If you want to improve as a person, then you should start competing with yourself and try to get better each day rather than seeing what others are doing. Once you start competing with yourself, your confidence level grows because you start feeling like a better person with every stepping stone and it makes you more positive in your approach as well. This confidence will continue to grow on a daily basis.

## Start Getting Active

Being active is a great way to boost your confidence and this is just because it's so much fun to do. Getting active does not necessarily mean heading to the gym and lifting unnecessary weights that make your arms and back ache like crazy. Getting active is all about indulging in outdoor activities you enjoy and this could be anything from going for a swim to cycling or even playing lawn tennis at your local club. If you are in the mood for dance, you should even enroll for a dance class just to see whether or not you have two left feet. If you manage to dance amazing, it will be a talent that you'll always cherish and want to look back and laugh at. It's important for you to understand that you may not be good at everything but trying a few new things won't harm you in anyway. When it comes to getting active you may want to do something that you enjoy because it's something that you should do on a regular basis. Any sort of exercise helps to release negative energy from your body and has a lot of positive impacts in your life. Not only do you start feeling more confident but you start enjoying yourself everyday which is essential for you to stay productive.

## Do What You Enjoy

Apart from the outdoor physical activities that help you stay healthy and positive; you should also make time to indulge in a hobby you enjoy. If you like cooking, make time to prepare a home cooked meal for your loved ones at least once in a week. Cooking is a great way to release a lot of your stress and it also helps you to connect with your loved ones a little more. If you're not a good cook it doesn't matter, you can still do something you enjoy such as painting, something crafty, or even collecting stamps for that matter. Repeating something over and over again is healthy because it makes you improve every time you do it and this encourages you to feel better about yourself. Once you do this, your confidence level starts to increase.

## Inspire Yourself

Confidence is something that will come from within so you need to learn how to generate self-confidence by inspiring yourself on a regular basis. It's funny how one simple positive quote can change your entire day and make you feel more confident than ever before. If you tried reading a positive motivational quote and it worked in your favor you may want to consider downloading a mobile app that can send you these positive quotes on a daily basis. There are tons of videos you can watch online as well to increase your confidence level and feel good about yourself. You just need to find what works well and stick to it. While most people find positive motivational quotes highly helpful there are some that find solace by simply hearing the voice of a loved one.

If you are romantically involved with somebody make time to talk to them about something positive every day before you head out to work and you will realize that your days are a lot better. If someone who is not close to you picks up the phone, have a few words with them. Try to make this a regular routine. There are different things that work for different people and spirituality it is also something that plays a huge role for a few. If you realize that by saying a short prayer every day your confidence is increasing - Do it. You can choose to do anything that works to you.

The key to becoming a confident person is to constantly try something new every time. Albert Einstein once wisely said "Insanity is doing the same thing over and over again and expecting different results". If you are looking to change or you are looking be a better person then the important thing you need to do is to learn how to push yourself and try new things every once in a while. You may be surprised at the number of changes you will introduce into your life and how confident you will become.

# Chapter 12:
# Persuade People Even When You're Nervous

Sometimes you find yourself in situations where it is difficult for you to open up and talk to people around you. While you will be able to work your way through this problem it's not something you can deal with immediately so you have to understand how essential it is for you to take one step at a time. There are various tips and tricks that you can apply to your life. When it comes to overcoming social awkwardness, you can still be confident among people with a little effort.

The first step you have to take to believe that you will be able to persuade people in the worst of situations is to believe that you are not boring. Most introverts believe that they should not talk much because they often believe that their conversations will bore peoplc. The truth is that none of your conversations can bore someone because every conversation you start is something that is relevant to you and you are highly interested in. Introverts do not like to indulge in unnecessary chatting. They always come up with thing things to discuss. No matter how nervous you are you should always try to begin a conversation because the chances that someone will not like what you started discussing is very slim.

Another reason why lots of introverts try to stay as quiet as possible is because they think that they are being judged. This is something you have to understand; people are not trying to judge you but rather they are trying to get to know you because they don't know you as well as they know an extrovert. Instead of letting that get to you, it's better to make an effort to try and talk to the people you believe do not know you. It is very difficult for you to begin a conversation when you feel that you are being judged but the minute you make an effort to begin talking you will realize that no one is looking at you in a negative way.

Even if someone is judging you, it is something you should not worry about because you can't control the way people think about you and it's not going to affect how well you do in life. Do not let somebody else's interference affect your success or come in the way of what you plan on getting done. You should do what you believe is right irrespective of what people around you have to say, so stop thinking about the world and begin thinking about how you will do things in the right way.

Being rejected by society is another unnecessary worry amongst introverts which prevents them from beginning a discussion or talking to the people they find interesting. You have to understand if you want to become successful, you will have to make an effort and even if somebody does not like you or rejects you it's not going to be as devastating as you think it will be. If anything, it will be a learning chapter in your life and you learn exactly how to deal with this situation in a better way the next time. Just because someone doesn't like your ideologies or ideas does not make you a bad person or make you worse than your competitors. It simply means that they do not understand your methodology and you have to try different approaches to help them to understand.

You also need to keep reminding yourself that what others think about you will not define who you are and the only person who can truly define what you represent is yourself. You have to let people know what you think and how you see society so that you will manage to perform better and more effectively. You also need to remember that nothing is really black and white. There are multiple shades of grey that come in between black and white that can also help define yourself.

## People do not Always Think About You

When you are an introvert and you are going through a bad day the major thing that you constantly worry about is that people are talking about you and thinking about your actions. Let's get one thing straight - everyone has their own life to worry about and their own problems to deal with so it's really rare for somebody to spend a lot of time pondering about what mistakes you made. You have to remember that social interactions barely have any effect on a person. Once the interactions are over and the only one who will be worrying about a certain conversation that happened in the past is you. Remember that people don't have a lot of time to judge you, so you have to let it go and even if the conversation was a horrible and horrendous conversation it's not something that you should worry about because the other person isn't thinking about it right now. If it was a completely embarrassing situation and you know people will talk about it, you can still save yourself a little grace because you will just be the talk of town for a few days and then people will find something new to talk about. Whether or not people are talking about you or thinking about you, you need to understand it's not going to affect you in any way.

## People are Also as Awkward as You are

If you thought that you are the most awkward person in the room you are actually mistaken. Extroverts also tend to feel awkward or socially anxious in certain situations so you are never alone. Somebody who is standing with a big smile slapped across the face could be just as nervous as you are and they could be pretending to be confident. Remember how we discussed trying to pretend to be confident? This is probably a good time for you to apply that theory and behave as though you are confident even though you are really nervous inside. Once you start doing this you will manage to put yourself in situations you are not really comfortable in. Apart from helping you feel more confident about yourself you will learn to take one step at a time. You will be comfortable to face social awkwardness with a confident approach. Do not let awkwardness get the better of you. You need to learn how to keep it in control so you can persuade people into liking you and letting them know that you're here to stay.

## People Are More Tolerant Than You Think

You may end up saying something that's embarrassing and horrifying but it's ok. You may believe that people are going to judge you but the truth is that they will not. People are more tolerant than you give them credit for and they may not even remember what you said or did to make a joke about it. Everyone goes through mishaps in their life and while some of them may be extremely difficult to deal with it, you to remember that you need to let it go and move on.

The minute you learn how to accept yourself for who you are, you will stop scrutinizing and judging everything that you do and every word you say. This will help you to deal with your anxiety in a more effective way and you will stop worrying about whether or not you are socially awkward. In all probability you are not, but even if you are it doesn't really matter because the people who will get to know you will like you for who you are and will remind you of what you say. When you have a certain amount of people you trust, they accept you completely - quirks and all. So, stop holding back just because you think you are not going to be liked.

## People Will Like You Even When You are not Perfect

You don't have to be the perfect person for somebody to like you or to establish relationships with, whether it's professional or personal.

Imperfections are just as beautiful and they are accepted irrespective of what you think. Just because someone has seen your inabilities does not make you a small person but rather it helps you to be more beautiful and also gives you the scope to learn to grow. When you let people in on your insecurities and weaknesses there is a strong possibility, they can help you overcome them and learn a better technique to deal with it rather than try to cover it up. You should never be apologetic of who you are or try to hide your flaws from the world.

## You Should Make Mistakes - It's Fine

If you keep telling yourself that you shouldn't make mistakes then you will end up making more mistakes than ever. Everyone is human and it is only human to make mistakes. So, don't be afraid if you make a few mistakes along the way - it is part of your journey. The minute you learn how to accept the mistakes you made, you realize that you are getting better at it and you are also improving on the kind of job that you do. When you think about situations with a clear head it helps you to get better at your task and this will lower the number of mistakes you make rather than increase them which is most important.

## Don't Self Evaluate

The biggest mistake introverts tend to make is they self-evaluate themselves and believe that they are worthless because they can't handle certain aspects of life. Don't do this because it's not right and it will make you go through a negative phase in life which will put you down. You need to accept that everyone cannot do everything and there are certain things you will do better than the others, while there will be things that they will be better at. Make sure you take your time to understand what you can do well and focus on getting that done rather than trying to do something you may not be able to do well. There is no harm in learning new things. However, you should focus on what you are highly skilled at while learning something new in the background.

## Face Your Social Fears

While you are ready train yourself to be present at social gathering it's now time to take a step ahead in these gatherings and make yourself more comfortable. Instead of standing in the corner at a party you may want to bring yourself towards the center one step at a time and meet people whom you may not have met in the past. Begin by introducing yourself and asking them questions about themselves. Follow the same techniques you would follow to break the ice with people at work. You can also begin to initiate a conversation with a few people you feel comfortable with. In case you can't start a conversation, you can always join one that you think is more approachable. Remember when you are trying to face your social fears do not put too much pressure on yourself but rather try to go with the flow. Most of the time you won't have to do a lot of work and you will realize that you have automatically taken every step that's required in order for you to be an active social member of a party.

While this may seem extremely difficult when you are nervous but with a little effort and smart approach, not only will you be able to overcome the awkwardness but you'll also start feeling more comfortable talking to a stranger under a pressure situation.

## Chapter 13:
## Understanding Other People's Emotions and Thrive

When you are an introvert it becomes very difficult for you to understand how to express yourself but the one thing that you will be a pro at will be to understand what other people are feeling and be more sensitive towards them. Introverts are highly elusive and they spend a lot of time analyzing people. This is why they are more sensitive and they manage to have a higher emotional intelligence in comparison to an extrovert. While emotional intelligence is something that you can achieve, the level of emotional intelligence in an introvert is already high and all they need to do is learn how to channel their energy into learning something new to use to their benefit. The more connected you are with your emntional intelligence the better it works for you and for the people around you. Once they learn how to master emotional intelligence, they manage to achieve something that adds meaning to their life, which can be used professionally and personally. Here we look at the five aspects of emotional intelligence and the elements in each of them.

## Self-Awareness

One of the best things about being emotionally intelligent is that you are able to identify your weakness and your strength and you also learn how to deal with it more effectively. It also gives you the confidence to learn how to accept your flaws and forgive anybody who may make fun of you. When you learn not to get affected by what people have to say, it starts to build a lot of confidence in you and this works wonders for introverts.

## #1 - Self-Knowledge

One of the best things of being emotionally intelligent is that you understand your personality, you build up your skills, and you know exactly how to act upon them when required. When you know yourself, you don't underestimate yourself and you are not over confident which helps you to make the right decisions in life.

## #2 - Accurate Self-Assessment

An introvert who is emotionally intelligent manages to self-assess themselves more confidently. They also know how to handle interactions and when they get uncomfortable, they know exactly when to drift away from those conversations which helps them to deal with the situation that much better.

## #3 - Self-Confidence

The more emotionally intelligent you are, the more you understand your self-worth which helps to build confidence.

## #4 - Emotional Awareness

When you have strong emotional intelligence, you are aware about what's happening around you and you also know how to acknowledge your feelings which makes a lot of difference with regards to the decisions you take.

## Self-Regulation

Emotional intelligence also comprises of self-regulation which is an integral part of an introvert gaining confidence. Apart from helping you to manage your emotions it also helps to keep your stress levels in control. It also works wonders to control your impulses that are usually responsible for the wrong decision that you end up making.

### #1 - Emotional Self-Control

When you learn how to control your emotions, it brings self-control and this ensures that you do not make impulsive decisions that turn out the wrong way. It also ensures that you do not stay in a negative state of mind for a longer time.

### #2 - Integrity

One of the most important values of being emotionally intelligent is integrity. It helps you to enhance your personal performance and learn how to trust yourself as well as others. It gives you a feeling of responsibility and makes you understand how essential it is for you to stay truthful. This ensures that you make the right decision instead of choosing to do something that is not morally right.

## #3 - Adaptability

One of the best things about being emotionally intelligent is that it helps you to learn how to adapt to changing situations and this is one of the best methods for an introvert to learn how to grow.

## #4 - Conscientiousness

If you want to make sure that you understand the job at hand and you get it done in an efficient and organized manner then your emotional intelligence plays a huge role in determining how you will sort it out.

# Motivation

Even when you are an introvert your emotional intelligence can help you to motivate yourself and become passionate about whatever you do. It helps you to look at situations from an optimistic perspective and this works well when it comes to achieving something in your personal or in your professional life.

## #1 - Achievement Drive

Emotional intelligence plays a huge role in helping you to strive to meet standards of excellence and this not only pushes you to achieve your goals better but it also ensures that you stay persistent with what you do.

## #2 - Commitment

One of the best things about being emotionally intelligent is that you learn how to commit to certain situations and follow up with it. When you are an introvert you tend to learn to make yourself comfortable with the commitment and this helps you to push a little harder.

### #3 - Initiative

One of the best things about being emotionally intelligent is that you are always willing to identify solutions for different opportunities and you also possess the ability to try out something new even when you are not confident about it or you are a little shy.

### #4 - Optimism

The best part about being emotionally intelligent is that you have a positive attitude towards various things that you do. It is important to have a positive attitude towards any steps that he or she is taking because this is what enables them to push a little harder every time and attempt to do something, they never thought possible.

### #5 - Learning Orientation

Apart from making a commitment about things that they want to complete; an introvert also learns how to focus and continuously make way for improvement when they are emotionally intelligent.

## Empathy

One of the best things about being emotionally intelligent and being an introvert is that your empathy is right up there and you automatically learn to be kind to other people. Apart from being a pro at listening to the problems you also try to help them figure out solutions.

### #1 - Understanding What Others Are Going Through

Being sensitive and putting yourself in another person's shoes is something that only an emotionally intelligent person can do and introverts manage to do this really well. They also put a lot of efforts into finding solutions to help deal with problems.

### #2 - Service Orientation

You learn how to anticipate what the people are looking for and help them to find it in order for them to do better, not only in the workplace but also in their personal life. Contributing towards a common goal or contributing towards something that is good is common for intelligent introverts.

### #3 - Appreciating Diversity

One of the best things about being emotionally intelligent and being an introvert is that you learn how to appreciate diversity which is not everybody's cup of tea. Whether it is dealing with people who belong to different economic backgrounds, nationalities, or even gender, it is always easier to do it when you are emotionally intelligent.

## Social Skills

There is no denying that introverts lack social skills but when they gain emotional intelligence, they are able to spruce up their social skills a lot better and learn how to use it to their advantage.

### #1 - Communication

An emotionally intelligent introvert not only spends a lot of time listening to what others have to say but they pay careful attention to every little detail which helps them to come up with solutions rather than just listening to them and not having anything to offer in return.

## #2 - Developing Others

One of the best things about an emotionally intelligent introvert is that they help to develop others by contributing their knowledge towards creating a better background and skill for them. Whether it is coaching them into doing something more effective or helping them spruce up their skills emotionally intelligent introverts are always at it.

## #3 - Collaboration

It is a lot easier to work with an emotionally intelligent introvert to collaborate and get the job done without having to face too many problems.

## #4 - Dealing with Conflict

Emotionally intelligent introverts try to resolve issues rather than create more and this helps them to negotiate and deal with the conflict rather than blow it up into an unnecessary problem.

# Chapter 14:
# Tips for the Sensitive and Shy

An introvert is always referred to as the one who is shy and sensitive and there is no denying that most of these traits are common with a lot of introverts out there. If you are wondering how you can deal with some of your problems, here are the most common questions that introverts often have in their head.

## How Do I Get Better?

It's only natural for an introvert to constantly wonder how he or she is going to get better and whether or not they are ever going to be able to be socially active without feeling awkward.

The truth is that you can get better as long as you put in a little effort and you begin by taking the very first step of doing something that you are not comfortable with. As mentioned in the book, the minute you learn how to make a list of the things that you are uncomfortable with and learn how to deal with them one step at a time, you will manage to overcome your social anxiety and fear and you will eventually get better. This may take a few days for some, while others may require weeks or even months to learn how to deal with it but you will get there.

## How Do I Take the First Step Towards Overcoming My Introvert Nature?

You don't have to overcome your introverted nature. You just need to learn how to live with it and make the most of it in a way that can prove to be beneficial to you. Throughout the book there are a number of tips and tricks that you can try and see whichever one works best for you. You need to understand that when it comes to overcoming your shyness or being able to get comfortable in a room full of strangers, you have to put in certain efforts and challenge yourself to do it even though you are not confident about how it will turn out.

## Is Being Introvert and Being Shy the Same Thing?

The truth is that an introvert doesn't necessarily have to be shy and a shy person doesn't necessarily have to be an introvert. An introvert is the person who may find it difficult to talk to a large crowd of people or speak in front of too many people they do not know that well. An introvert may not necessarily be shy. They may be outgoing and fun loving in front of their special few people they are comfortable with. A shy person, on the other hand, does not open up to the public and no matter how close they are to someone they will still have the traits of being shy.

## How Do I Acknowledge My Fear?

This is a big step for introverts because it is difficult to acknowledge what you are scared of and then start to face it. If you are scared of being in a room full of strangers you need to understand why you are scared in the first place. What triggers your anxiety and what makes you feel like you will not be able to survive. Figure out why you are scared and you will then manage to address the fear and then learn how to deal with it. You have to understand what causes your fear if you want the fear to go away.

## What If I Make Mistakes?

It's common to make a lot of mistakes along the way and there's nothing wrong with it. All you need to understand is that you have to stay accountable for the mistakes you make because it is only then that you will begin to learn how to change your attitude towards society and improve on your social interaction. While some days may be great, there may be times that you would wish you could go back home and never step back out again, but you have to understand that the good comes with the bad and it is important for you to face the bad just as efficiently as you accept the good.

## What If I'm Upset?

As much as we would like to believe that an introvert is generally a calm person who does not lose their temper, the truth is introverts can also be hot tempered and in case you are upset about something, the last thing you want to do is have an outburst in front of people. Considering you don't talk much; an outburst is not acceptable so you have to learn how to stay calm and try to lighten the mood the minute you get upset. You should also try to divert your attention to things that you actually like so that you forget about why you were absent in the first place. If it is not helping, the best thing to do is think back on happy memories from your childhood and see what a difference it makes to your mindset.

## How Do I Deal with Stage Fright?

Stage fright is more common than you think and as an introvert it is something that you have to learn to cope with especially if you plan on becoming a successful entrepreneur. If you are not comfortable with taking your first steps in front of a crowd and you know that you are going to freeze, you may want to start by releasing web-based versions see how people react to it. You can also ask your family members or your best friends to help you. While a mirror will help you gain confidence, you may or may not be able to face a crowd of people staring back at you. Start slow with a small group of around three or four people and move forward from them. Be prepared for honest feedback from your practice group because this will help you overcome your fright.

## What If I Know the Answer but I Am Too Afraid to Speak?

This is a common problem introvert's face and in case you find it difficult to speak to people or reply to somebody even though you know the answer because you are not familiar with them, you may want to start practicing by looking in the mirror. If there have been multiple meetings where you found yourself dumbstruck just because you couldn't reply to certain questions then you need to start having a conversation with yourself in front of the mirror because believe it or not, this gives you a lot of confidence. If you are still not sure how you can build your confidence, you can even speak with your best friend and see his or her reaction. Ask them to be honest with you with their feedback.

## How Do I Deal with A Loss of Energy?

Introverts tend to lose out on energy a lot faster in comparison to an extrovert because they end up using a lot of energy communicating when they were not comfortable doing so. If you realize that you are at a stage in your day where you are going to feel completely drained then you may want to take a break of silence or disconnect from people for a while till you recharge yourself. As an introvert you should constantly recharge yourself from time to time because this helps you feel energized and you will be able to deal with the day better and tackle uncomfortable situations efficiently. You can also try and do something that will help recharge you faster. This could be anything like listening to music or just picking up the phone and speaking to a loved one. It is important that you disconnect from the rest of the elements that are causing your energy to drain out.

## What If I Am Not Interested in A Conversation?

It's very common for introverts to feel bored in a conversation that doesn't include them and, in such situations, the smartest way for you to deal with it is to be honest and transparent about your opinion. If they are discussing something that is not related to your work or something you have no clue about, you can always ask to be excused by saying you have other things to do and let them know that the conversation does not interest you in any way. It is important for you to let people know what conversations interest you and what don't interest you because they will not try and make an attempt to talk about things that don't interest you in future. While others may think that you are rude, there is no point worrying about what they may think. Your time is precious and you need to make it clear to people that you would rather spend your time doing something productive.

## Is Something Wrong with Me?

Introverts often feel that there is something wrong with them because they can't deal with social situations and they look at all the other extroverts out there who are blending in with the crowd as seamlessly as possible. There is nothing wrong with you and it's just who you are, so your social anxiety and fear are normal. You just need to learn how to deal with them so that it doesn't affect your personal or professional life in anyway. Do not let anyone else put you down. You need to be confident in your abilities and do not let self-doubt creep in.

## How Do I Approach Uncomfortable Situations?

When you know that there is an uncomfortable situation you need to approach, it's important to prepare yourself for it in advance. You also need to try and keep a backup for the plan because this is what will help you deal with the situation in a better way and ensure that there is nothing that can go wrong. For example, if you have to head to a party that you dread, keep a backup in the form of a friend calling you up, and asking you to rush back home. You need to make sure that you think of such situations in advance so that it looks natural and the host of the party will not feel bad about you leaving abruptly.

## What If I Start A Conversation and I Am Not Comfortable with It?

While this will rarely happen but if it does, all you need to do is try to end the conversation without being abrupt. When you strike a conversation with someone and you find the conversation uncomfortable there is a strong chance the person who is having the conversation with you will find it just as awkward. So, if you try to stop the conversation, they will not want to continue it and will end it from their side as well. Do not be afraid of being judged because that is not going to be the case at all. People have a lot on their plate and the last thing they would want to do is judge you when you are ending an uncomfortable conversation.

You need to keep reminding yourself that there are a number of socially awkward people around you and just because you are an introvert does not make you a different person from the rest of the crowd. You are like every other person out there with your own differences that you are learning to deal with. The minute you learn to accept who you are and understand what you need to change in order to be a better person, not only will you lead a happy life but you will also lead a more successful one.

**If you find this book helpful in anyway a review to support my endeavors is much appreciated.**

**Samuel C. Larson**

How Quiet Introverts Thrive in An Extrovert World

www.ingramcontent.com/pod-product-compliance
Lightning Source LLC
Chambersburg PA
CBHW060455080526
44584CB00015B/1442